CW00925380

GASTON BACHELARD

THE POETICS
OF *R*EVERIE

CHILDHOOD, LANGUAGE, AND THE COSMOS

Translated from the French by Daniel Russell

BEACON PRESS ✌ BOSTON

La Poétique de la Rêverie
© 1960 by Presses Universitaires de France
Translation © 1969 by Grossman Publishers, Inc.
All rights reserved

International Standard Book Number: 0-8070-6413-0
First published as a Beacon Paperback in 1971 by arrangement
  with Grossman Publishers, Inc.

Beacon Press books are published under the auspices of the
  Unitarian Universalist Association
Printed in the United States of America
24 23   20 19 18

Translator's Preface

Men have always fashioned reveries out of sights and sounds, odors and memories. Indeed, reverie is such a common and even characteristic phenomenon of human nature that one may well wonder why it has not more often been the subject of scrutiny, description and analysis. Some of the reasons for this curious neglect may help explain the difficulties encountered in translating into English a discussion of reverie such as we find in this book by Gaston Bachelard.

Reverie has traditionally been understood, especially in the United States, to be unproductive, impractical and so completely unempirical as to be considered almost immoral in a society oriented toward pure and sometimes mindless action. The communication of reveries is, of course, possible through the language of poetry, but the English language used in social and intellectual transactions within the context of contemporary Anglo-Saxon culture is poorly suited to the inspection and discussion of all that is unempirical. Not only have we Anglo-Saxons lost our genders, but because of our life style and attitude toward the everyday manifestations of the imagination, we have also become inattentive to the immensely rich resonances of conceits and the profound analogies to be felt in the verbal or visual resemblances of puns. The difference between the French and English languages and the resulting divergence of thought patterns in the two different cultures become abundantly clear as we read this extraordinary book. But since conceits and puns translate so poorly, since gender reveries can hardly be translated at all, the reader will have difficulty appreciating the enormously rich potential of Bachelard's phenomenological method for the investigation of reverie. He should, however, become increasingly aware of the immense value of reverie and see how to make use of his own reverie in reading the poets with a new feeling of solidarity reaching far beyond the traditional forms of banal comprehension.

A discussion of reverie is not easy even in the language in which the reverie took form. It is inseparable from the personal past of memories and images which belongs only to the dreamer, and each word he uses is colored by this past. And since a reverie, as Bachelard suggests, is inseparable as well from the language in which it was dreamed, a translation is especially difficult. The very nature of the dreamer's language has shaped the reverie. So when a discussion or account of reveries is translated, the peculiarities of the original language must somehow be circumvented. That is why I have often been forced, in the course of this translation, to give the gender of French words and even the French words themselves on occasions when those words cast spells by their shape and sound as well as by their multiplicity of interacting meanings. Double meanings had to be explained in notes to alert the reader to puns and conceits. And, in some cases, I made no effort to translate, letting the reader discover the meaning of a word like *chosier* from the context as most French readers too would be obliged to do. Generally, these words refer to such a uniquely regional or personal reality as to be utterly untranslatable into English.

Such explanatory devices were used as sparingly as possible and were intended to remain unobtrusive, but they were, it seems to me, necessary to make my description of Bachelard's undertaking as clear and precise as possible. This word "description" may be disconcerting when used to refer to what is generally called a translation. But when one wishes to render a verbal creation (as opposed to a didactic statement) from one language to another, he is confronted with two equally unsatisfactory choices. He may, according to his talents, elaborate a similar, but never identical creation, or he may describe that creation as completely as possible

in his own language. I have chosen to "describe" Gaston Bachelard's inquiry into the nature and uses of reverie and have used
the devices of notes and parentheses to make my "description"
as objective, as clear, as impersonal, as photographic if you will,
as possible. It is hoped that such attempted objectivity will faithfully present not only the method and the thought but the man
as well, in all his articulate complexity, in all his wealth of human
understanding.

Daniel Russell
Pittsburgh
May 20, 1969

Contents

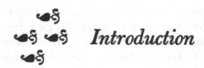

Introduction

Method, Method, what do you want from me?
You know that I have eaten of the fruit of the subconscious.
                    Jules Laforgue, *Moralités légendaires*

I

In previous works devoted to the poetic imagination, we have
tried to show the value of phenomenological method. The importance of such phenomenological inquiries lies in the complete illumination of the awareness of a subject who is struck with
wonder by poetic images. This awareness, which modern phenomenology tends to associate with all the other phenomena of
the psyche, seems to us to give a durable, subjective value to images which often have only a doubtful or ephemeral objectivity.
By obliging us to retrace our steps systematically and make an
effort toward clarity of awareness with respect to a poet's given
image, the phenomenological method leads us to attempt communication with the creating consciousness of the poet. The new-
born poetic image—a simple image!—thus becomes quite simply
an absolute origin, an origin of consciousness. In times of great
discoveries, a poetic image can be the seed of a world, the seed of
a universe imagined out of a poet's reverie. The consciousness of
wonder blossoms forth in all innocence before this world which

has been created by the poet. There is no doubt that consciousness is destined for greater exploits. It manifests itself more strongly as it turns to ever more highly coordinated works. In particular, the "consciousness of rationality" has a quality of permanence which poses a difficult problem for the phenomenologist: he is obliged to explain how various moments of consciousness are connected in a chain of truths. But, at least at first glance, the imagining consciousness, in opening out on an isolated image, has more limited responsibilities. The imagining consciousness, then, when it is considered in relation to separate or isolated images, might contribute themes to an elementary pedagogical system for phenomenological doctrines.

But here we are faced with a double paradox. The uninitiated reader will ask why we overload a book on reverie with the heavy philosophical apparatus of the phenomenological system.

For his part, the professional phenomenologist will ask why we choose a subject as fluid and unstable as imagery to display and demonstrate the phenomenological principles.

It might perhaps be simpler if we were to follow the tried and true methods of the psychologist who describes what he observes, measures levels, and classifies types—who sees imagination being born in children without ever really examining how it dies in ordinary men.

But can a philosopher become a psychologist? Can he bend his pride to the point of contenting himself with the notation of facts when he has already entered with all requisite passion into the realm of values? A philosopher remains, as they say today, "in a philosophical situation"; occasionally he pretends to begin everything at the beginning, but, alas! he continues . . . He has read so many books of philosophy! Under the pretext of studying and teaching them, he has deformed so many "systems!" And when evening has come and he is no longer teaching, he believes he has the right to shut himself up in the system of his choice.

And thus it is that I have chosen phenomenology in hopes of reexamining in a new light the faithfully beloved images which are so solidly fixed in my memory that I no longer know whether I am remembering or imagining them when I come across them in my reveries.

II

Furthermore, the phenomenological requirement with respect to poetic images is simple: it returns to putting the accent on their original quality, grasping the very essence of their originality and thus taking advantage of the remarkable psychic productivity of the imagination.

The requirement that the poetic image be a source of psychic activity would, however, appear excessively harsh were we not able to find an element of originality even in the variations at work on the most strongly rooted archetypes. Since it has been our intention to delve more deeply into the psychology of wonder from the phenomenological point of view, the least variation in a wonder-filled image ought to help refine our inquiry. The subtlety of an innovation revives the source, renews and redoubles the joy of wonder.

In poetry, wonder is coupled with the joy of speech. This joy must be considered in its absolute positiveness appearing as a new being in language. The poetic image is in no way comparable, as with the mode of the common metaphor, to a valve which would open up to release pent-up instincts. The poetic image sheds light on consciousness in such a way that it is pointless to look for subconscious antecedents of the image. Phenomenology, at least, is set up to consider the poetic image in its own being, distinct and independent from any antecedent being, as a positive conquest of the word. If one were to listen to the psychoanalyst, he would come to define poetry as a majestic Lapsus of the Word. But man is not deceived by becoming exalted. Poetry is one of the destinies of speech. In trying to sharpen the awareness of language at the level of poems, we get the impression that we are touching the man whose speech is new in that it is not limited to expressing ideas or sensations, but tries to have a future. One would say that the poetic image, in its newness, opens a future to language.

Correlatively, by using the phenomenological method in the examination of poetic images, it has seemed to us that we were being automatically psychoanalyzed and that we might, with a clear conscience, repress our former obsessions with psychoanalytic culture. As a phenomenologist, we have felt liberated from those of our preferences which transform literary taste into habit. Because of the privileged position which phenomenology gives the present, we have been ready to welcome with open arms the new images offered by the poet. The image was present, present in us and separated from all that past which might have prepared it in the soul of the poet. Without worrying about the poet's "complexes," without rummaging about in the history of his life, we were free, systematically free, to pass from one poet to another, from a great poet to a minor poet with regard to a simple image which would reveal its poetic worth precisely through its wealth of variations.

Thus the phenomenological method would enjoin us to display the entire consciousness at the origin of the least variation in the image. One doesn't read poetry while thinking of other things. As soon as a poetic image renews itself in any single one of its traits, it manifests a primitive simplicity.

It is this simplicity, systematically revealed, which ought to result in a pure reception of the poems. In our studies of the active imagination, we shall follow phenomenology then as a school of naïveté.

III

Faced with images which the poets bring us, faced with images which we could never have imagined ourselves, this naïveté of wonderment is completely natural. But in submitting passively to such wonder, one does not participate profoundly enough in the creating imagination. The phenomenology of the image requires that we participate actively in the creating imagination. Since the goal of all phenomenology is to situate awareness in the present, in a moment of extreme tension, we are forced to conclude that, in so far as the characteristics of the imagination are concerned, there is no phenomenology of passivity. In light of the commonly held misconception, let us recall that phenomenology does not involve an empirical description of phenomena. Empirical description involves enslavement to the object by decreeing passivity on the part of the subject. The psychologist's description can doubtless add documentation, but the phenomenologist must intervene to set this documentation on the axis of intentionality.

Ah! if only this image which has just been given to me could be mine, really mine, if it could become—height of a reader's vanity!—my creation! And what a glorious experience reading would be if I could live out, with the poet's help, *poetic intentionality!* It is through the intentionality of poetic imagination that the poet's soul discovers the opening of consciousness common to all true poetry.

In encountering such limitless ambition, together with the fact that our entire book must emerge from our reveries, our phenomenological enterprise must face up to a radical paradox. Reverie is commonly classified among the phenomena of psychic détente. It is lived out in a relaxed time which has no linking force. Since it functions with inattention, it is often without memory. It is a flight from out of the real that does not always find a consistent unreal world. By following "the path of reverie"—a constantly downhill path—consciousness relaxes and wanders and consequently *becomes clouded.* So it is never the right time, when one is dreaming, to "do phenomenology."

What is our attitude to be in the face of such a paradox? Instead of attempting to reconcile the terms of the obvious antithesis between a simply psychological study of reverie and a properly phenomenological study, we shall heighten the contrast futher by placing our research under the auspices of a philosophical thesis which we would first like to defend. In our view any awareness is an increment to consciousness, an added light, a reinforcement of psychic coherence. Its swiftness or instantaneity can hide this growth from us. But there is a growth of being in every instance of awareness. Consciousness is in itself an act, the human act. It is a lively, full act. Even if the action which follows, which ought to have followed or should have followed, remains in suspense, the consciousness-as-act is still completely positive or kinetic. In the present essay we shall study this act only in the realm of language and more precisely yet in poetic language when the imagining consciousness creates and lives the poetic image. Adding to language, creating from language, stabilizing and loving language, are all activities where the consciousness of speaking is increased. Within this narrowly limited domain, we are certain to find numerous examples which prove our more general philosophical thesis on the essentially augmentative potential of all awareness.

But then, in the face of this accentuation of the clarity and vigor of the poetic awareness, from what angle must we study reverie in order to take advantage of the lessons of Phenomenology? For actually our own philosophical thesis adds to the difficulty of our problem. In fact, this thesis has a corollary: a consciousness which diminishes, which goes to sleep, a consciousness which *daydreams* (*rêvasse*) is no longer a consciousness. Reverie puts us on the wrong path, the downhill path.

An adjective is going to save everything and permit us to go on to the objections of a superficial psychology. The reverie we intend to study is *poetic* reverie. This is a reverie which poetry puts on the right track, the track an expanding consciousness follows. This reverie is written, or, at least, promises to be written. It is already facing the great universe of the blank page. Then images begin to compose and fall into place. The dreamer is already hearing the sounds of written words. An author, whose name escapes me, used to say that the pen point was an extension of the mind. I am completely convinced of it: when my pen leaks, I think awry. And who will give me back the good ink of my school days?

All the senses awaken and fall into harmony in poetic reverie. Poetic reverie listens to this polyphony of the senses, and the poetic consciousness must record it. The poetic image is suited to what Friedrich Schlegel said of language: it is "spontaneous creation." [1] It is such *élans* of the imagination which the phenomenologist of imagination must try to revive.

Of course, a psychologist would find it more direct to study the inspired poet. He would make concrete studies of inspiration in individual geniuses. But for all that, would he experience the phenomena of inspiration? [2] His human documentation gathered from inspired poets could hardly be related, except from the exterior, in an ideal of objective observations. Comparison of inspired

---

[1] "Eine Hervorbringung im Ganzen." We are using Ernest Renan's fine translation. Cf. *De l'origine du langage,* 3rd edition, 1859. p. 100.
[2] "Poetry is something more than poets." George Sand, *Questions d'art et de littérature,* p. 283.

poets would soon make us lose sight of inspiration. Any comparison diminishes the expressive qualities of the terms of the comparison. The word "inspiration" is too general to express the originality of inspired words. Indeed, the psychology of inspiration, even when accounts of the "artificial paradises" come to our aid, is obviously meager. In such studies there are too few documents with which the psychologist can work, and above all, they are not really accepted as subject matter by the psychologist.

The notion of *Muse*, a notion which should help us *give body to* inspiration and which should make us believe that there is a transcendant subject for the verb *inspire*, cannot enter naturally into the vocabulary of a phenomenologist. Already as a very young adolescent, I could not understand how a poet whom I liked so much could use lutes and muses. How can you recite, with conviction and without breaking out laughing, this first line of a famous poem: "Poet, take your lute and give me a kiss?" It was more than a child of Champagne could bear.

No! Muse, Lyre of Orpheus, phantoms of hashish or opium can only conceal the *substance of inspiration* from us. Written poetic reverie, led to the point of producing a page of literature, will, on the contrary, become for us a transmittable reverie, an inspiring reverie, that is to say, an inspiration tailored to our talents as readers.

In this case, documents are abundant for a solitary, systematically solitary, phenomenologist. The phenomenologist can awaken his poetic consciousness at the contact of a thousand images which lie sleeping in books. He *reverberates* to the poetic image in the very sense of phenomenological resonance so well described by Eugene Minkowski.[8]

Furthermore, let us note that in contrast to a dream a reverie cannot be recounted. To be communicated, it must be *written*, written with emotion and taste, being relived all the more strongly because it is being written down. Here, we are touching the realm of *written love*. It is going out of fashion, but the benefits remain. There are still souls for whom love is the contact of two poetries, the fusion of two reveries. The epistolary novel ex-

---

8 Cf.. *The Poetics of Space*, (New York, 1964) Orion Press, p. 2.

presses love in a beautiful emulation of images and metaphors. To tell a love, one must write. One never writes too much. How many lovers, upon returning home from the tenderest of rendezvous, open their writing desks! Love is never finished expressing itself, and it expresses itself better the more poetically it is dreamed. The reveries of two solitary souls prepare the sweetness of loving. A realist of passion will see nothing there but evanescent formulas. But just the same it is no less true that great passions are prepared by great reveries. The reality of love is mutilated when it is detached from all its unrealness.

Under such conditions, it becomes immediately evident how complex and unstable will be any debate between a psychology of reverie based on the observation of dreamers and a phenomenology of the creating image which tends to restore, even to an average reader, the innovating action of poetic language. In a more general way, one can also understand the great value in establishing a phenomenology of the imaginary where the imagination is restored to its proper, all-important place as the principle of direct stimulation of psychic becoming. Imagination attempts to have a future. At first it is an element of imprudence which detaches us from heavy stabilities. We shall see that certain poetic reveries are hypothetical lives which enlarge our lives by letting us in on the secrets of the universe. A world takes form in our reverie, and this world is ours. This dreamed world teaches us the possibilities for expanding our being within our universe. There is *futurism* in any dreamed universe. Joé Bousquet wrote: "In a world born of him, man can become anything." [4]

Thenceforth, if you consider poetry in all its fire of human becoming, at the summit of an inspiration which delivers the new world to us, what can be the use of a biography which tells us the past, the heavy past of the poet? If we had the least inclination for polemic, what a dossier we could assemble on the subject of the excesses of biography. We shall give only a sample.

Half a century ago, a prince of literary criticism set himself the task of explicating Verlaine's poetry, which he liked very little. For how can one like the poetry of an artist who lives on the

[4] Quoted without reference by Gaston Puel in an article in *Le Temps et les hommes*, March, 1958, p. 62.

fringe of literate society: "No one has ever seen him either on the boulevards or at the theater or in a salon. He is somewhere at the other end of Paris, in a wine merchant's backroom drinking *vin bleu*."

Cheap wine! What a slight to the beaujolais they were drinking then in the little cafés of the *montagne* Sainte-Geneviève!

The same literary critic puts the finishing touches to the poet's character by describing his hat. He writes: "His slouch hat itself seemed to conform to his sad thought with its vague rim turned up all around his head like a kind of black halo for his troubled brow. His hat! And yet it too was joyful when it felt like it and capricious like a very dark woman. Sometimes it is round and naive like that of a child of Auvergne or Savoy; sometimes it perches on one ear like a tilted, dented Tyrolian cone. Or again it is facetiously terrible, like the headdress of some bandito, all askew, one side turned down, the other up, the front like a visor and the back down on the nape of his neck." [5]

Is there one single poem in all the work of the poet which can be explained by these literary contortions over the hat?

It is so difficult to link the life to the work! Can the biographer help us by telling us that the following poem was written while Verlaine was in prison at Mons:

> The sky is up above the roof
> So blue, so calm.

In prison! Who is not in prison in times of melancholy? In my room in Paris, far from the land of my birth, I carry on Verlaine's reverie. A sky from another time spreads out over the city of stone. And through my memory hum the bars of music that Reynaldo Hahn wrote to accompany Verlaine's poems. A whole layer of emotions, reveries and memories grows up out of this poem for me. Above the poem—not beneath in a life which I have not lived, not in the poorly lived life of the unhappy poet. Did not the work dominate his life; is not the work a pardon for the man who has lived badly?

In any event, it is in this sense that the poem can gather reveries and assemble dreams, songs, and memories.

---

[5] Quoted by Antheaume and Dromard, *Poésie et folie* (Paris, 1908), p. 351.

Psychological literary criticism directs us to other interests. It makes a man out of a poet. But in great poetical successes the problem remains intact: how can a man become a poet in spite of life?

But let us get back to our simple task of indicating the constructive character of poetic reverie. In order to prepare for this task, let us ask ourselves if reverie is in all circumstances a phenomenon of relaxation and abandon, as suggested by classical psychology.

IV

Psychology has more to lose than to gain if it forms its basic notions under the inspiration of etymological derivations. Etymology can minimize the clearest differences between dream (*rêve*)[6] and reverie. And further, since psychologists seize upon what is most characteristic, they study the astonishing nocturnal dream (*rêve*) first, and they pay little attention to the reveries which for them are only confused dreams without structure, history, or mystery. Reverie is, then, just a little nocturnal matter forgotten in the light of day. If the oneiric matter condenses a little in the soul of the dreamer, reverie falls into dream; the "gusts of reverie" noted by psychiatrists asphyxiate the psychism, the reverie becomes somnolence, and the dreamer falls asleep. Thus a sort of fatal fall marks the passage from reverie to dream. It is a poor reverie which invites a nap. One must even wonder whether, in this "falling asleep," the subconscious itself does not undergo a decline in being. The subconscious will continue its action in the dreams of real sleep. Psychology works toward the two poles of clear thought and nocturnal dream, and is thus certain of having under its purview the entire spectrum of the human psyche.

But there are other reveries which do not belong to this twi-

---

6 In French there are two words which mean "dream"—*rêve* and *songe*. Throughout this translation, I have generally indicated which word was translated as "dream" only when Bachelard wanted to stress the difference between two homophonic words or when *songe, songer, songeur*, etc. had been used in the French text (Translator's note).

light state where diurnal and nocturnal life mingle. And, in many respects, diurnal reverie deserves direct study. Reverie is a spiritual phenomenon which is too natural—and also too useful in psychic equilibrium—to be treated as a derivative of the dream or to be placed categorically in the order of oneiric phenomena. In short, in order to determine the essence of reverie, it is quite sufficient to return to reverie itself. And it is precisely by phenomenology that the distinction between dream and reverie can be clarified, since the possible intervention of consciousness in the reverie bears decisive significance.

One might wonder whether there really is a consciousness of dreams. A dream can be so strange that it seems that another subject has come to dream within us. "A dream visited me." That is certainly the formula which indicates the passivity of great nocturnal dreams. To convince ourselves that they are really ours, we must reinhabit these dreams. Afterwards we make up accounts of them, stories from another time, adventures from another world. The man who comes back from afar lies with impunity. Innocently, unconsciously, we often insert a detail which adds to the picturesqueness of our adventure in the realm of the night. Have you ever noticed the physiognomy of the man who is recounting his dream? He smiles at his drama, at his fears. He is amused and wants you to be amused.[7] The teller of dreams sometimes enjoys his dream as an original work. In it he experiences a delegated originality; and hence he is very much surprised when a psychoanalyst tells him that another dreamer has known the same "originality." The dream-dreamer's conviction of having lived the dream he is recounting must not deceive us. It is a reported conviction which is reinforced each time he retells the dream. There is certainly no identity between the subject who is telling and the subject who dreamed. For this reason, a really phenomenological elucidation of the nocturnal dream poses a difficult problem. One

---

[7] Very often, I confess, the teller of dreams bores me. His dream could perhaps interest me if it were frankly worked on. But to hear a glorious tale of his insanity! I have not yet clarified, psychoanalytically, this boredom during the recital of other people's dreams. Perhaps I have retained the stiffness of a rationalist. I do not follow the tale of justified incoherence docilely. I always suspect that part of the stupidities being recounted are invented.

would doubtless find elements useful in solving this problem if he further developed a psychology and, consecutively, a phenomenology of reverie.

Instead of looking for the dream in reverie, people should look for reverie in the dream. There are calm beaches in the midst of nightmares. Robert Desnos has noted the intrusion of dream and reverie upon each other: "Although sleepy and dreaming without being able to distinguish exactly between dream and reverie, I retain the notion of décor." [8] This is the same as saying that the dreamer comes upon the splendors of the day in the night of sleep. Then he is conscious of the beauty of the world. The beauty of the dream world returns his consciousness to him for an instant.

And thus it is that reverie illustrates repose for a being, that it illustrates well-being. The dreamer and his reverie enter totally into the substance of happiness. During a visit to Nemours in 1844, Victor Hugo had gone out at twilight "to go see a few bizarre paving stones." Night was coming, the city was quieting down. Where was the city?

All that was neither a city, nor a church, nor a river, nor color, nor light, nor shadow: it was reverie.

For a long time, I remained motionless, letting myself be penetrated gently by this unspeakable ensemble, by the serenity of the sky and the melancholy of the moment. I do not know what was going on in my mind, and I could not express it; it was one of those ineffable moments when one feels something in himself which is going to sleep and something which is awakening.[9]

Thus a whole universe comes to contribute to our happiness when reverie comes to accentuate our repose. You must tell the man who wants to dream well to begin by being happy. Then reverie plays out its veritable destiny; it becomes poetic reverie and by it, in it, everything becomes beautiful. If the dreamer had "the gift" he would turn his reverie into a work. And this work

---

[8] Robert Desnos, *Domaine public*. Gallimard, 1953, p. 38.
[9] Victor Hugo, *En voyage . . . France et Belgique*. In *L'homme qui rit* (vol. I, p. 148) Hugo writes: "The sea observed is a reverie."

chimeras. Whoever will agree to follow these chimeric indications and group his own reveries into reveries on reveries will find perhaps, at the bottom of the dream (*songe*), the great tranquility of the intimate feminine being. He will return to this gynaeceum of remembrances which comprises all memory, very ancient memory.

More positive than the first, our second chapter must nevertheless still be put under the general heading of "Reveries on Reverie." We shall use, as best we can, documents furnished by psychologists, but since we mix these documents with our own idea-dreams, it is suitable that we, as a philosopher who uses the knowledge of the psychologist, take full responsibility for our own aberrations.

The woman's situation in the modern world has been the object of much research. Books like those by Simone de Beauvoir and F. J. J. Buytendijk are analyses which get to the bottom of the problems.[13] In trying to indicate more precisely how the masculine and feminine—especially the feminine—help fashion our reveries, we are limiting our observations only to "oneiric situations."

We shall then borrow most of our arguments from the Psychology of the depths. In numerous works C. G. Jung has shown the existence of a profound duality in the human Psyche. He has situated this duality under the double sign of an *animus* and an *anima*. For him and for his disciples there may be found in any psychism, whether that of a man or a woman, an *animus* and an *anima*, sometimes cooperating, sometimes in dissonance. We shall not follow all the developments which the psychology of the depths has given to this theme of an intimate duality. We simply wish to show that reverie in its simplest and purest state belongs to the *anima*. Of course, any simplification runs the risk of mutilating reality; but it helps us establish perspectives. Let us say then, that in general the dream (*rêve*) issues from the *animus*, and reverie from the *anima*. Reverie without drama, without event or history gives us true repose, the repose of the feminine. There we gain gentleness of living. Gentleness, slowness, peace,

---

13 Simone de Beauvoir, *Le deuxième sexe*, Gallimard; F. J. J. Buytendijk, *La femme. Ses modes d'être, de paraître, d'exister.* Desclée de Brouwer, 1954.

such is the motto of reverie in *anima*. It is in reverie that we can find the fundamental elements for a philosophy of repose.

Our reveries, which lead us back to our childhood, gravitate toward the pole of the *anima*. These reveries toward childhood will be the subject of our third chapter. But, henceforth, we must indicate the angle from which we are going to study the memories of childhood.

In the course of earlier work we often stated that one could scarcely develop a psychology of the creative imagination if he did not succeed in distinguishing clearly between imagination and memory. If there is any realm where distinction is especially difficult, it is the realm of childhood memories, the realm of *beloved images* harbored in memory since childhood. These memories which live by the image and in virtue of the image become, at certain times of our lives and particularly during the quiet age, the origin and matter of a complex reverie: the memory dreams, and reverie remembers. When this reverie of remembering becomes the germ of a poetic work, the complex of memory and imagination becomes more tightly meshed; it has multiple and reciprocal actions which deceive the sincerity of the poet. More exactly, the happy childhood memories are told with a *poet's sincerity*. The imagination ceaselessly revives and illustrates the memory.

We shall try to present, in a condensed form, an ontological philosophy of childhood which underlines the durable character of childhood. By certain of its traits, *childhood lasts all through life*. It returns to animate broad sections of adult life. First, childhood never leaves its nocturnal retreats. Within us, a child sometimes comes to watch over us in our sleep. But in waking life itself, when reverie works on our history, the childhood which is within us brings us its benefits. One needs, and sometimes it is very good, to live with the child which he has been. From such living he achieves a consciousness of roots, and the entire tree of his being takes comfort from it. Poets will help us find this living childhood within us, this permanent, durable immobile world.

Here in our introduction we must already emphasize that in the chapter on "Reverie Toward Childhood," we are not setting up a child psychology. We envisage childhood only as a theme for reverie. This theme comes up in every age of life. We maintain ourselves in a reverie and in an *anima* meditation. Much different research would be necessary in order to shed light on the dramas of childhood and above all in order to show that these dramas do not disappear, but that they can be reborn, and indeed want to be reborn. Anger lasts; primitive anger awakens the sleeping childhood. Sometimes in our solitude these repressed bursts of anger nurture projects of vengeance and plans of crime. These are constructions of the *animus*. They are not the reveries of the *anima*. A different plan of inquiry would be necessary for examining them. But any psychologist studying the imagination of the drama must refer back to the childhood fits of anger and adolescent revolts. A psychologist of the depths like the poet Pierre-Jean Jouve does not fail to. Having to preface a group of stories he had entitled *Histoires sanglantes,* the poet, in a condensation of psychoanalytic culture, says that "states of childhood" are the basis of his stories.[14] Unfinished dramas produce works where the *animus* is active, clairvoyant, prudent, audacious and complex. Keeping strictly to our task of analyzing *reveries,* we shall leave aside the *animus projects.* Our chapter on reveries toward childhood then is simply a contribution to the metaphysics of the elegiac time. After all, this time of intimate elegy and lasting regret is a psychological reality. It is durable duration. Our chapter establishes itself as the working draft for a metaphysics of the unforgettable.

But it is difficult for a philosopher to tear himself away from his long time habits of thought. Even in writing a book on leisure, one's old words want to get into the act. So we believe we should write a chapter under a good pedantic title: "The *Cogito* of the Dreamer." Over my forty years as a philosopher, I have heard it said that philosophy got off to a new start with Descartes' *cogito ergo sum.* I too have probably pronounced this initial lesson. It is such a clear motto in the order of thought! But would we not be upsetting its dogmatism if we asked the dreamer whether he is quite sure of being the being who is dreaming his dream? Such a question would hardly trouble a Descartes. For him, thinking,

14 P.-J. Jouve, *Histoires sanglantes,* Gallimard, p. 16.

wishing, loving and dreaming are always activities of his mind. That fortunate man was sure that it was he, really he, and he alone who had passions and wisdom. But is a dreamer, a real dreamer who crosses the madnesses of the night, so sure of being himself? We doubt it. We have always retreated from the analysis of nocturnal dreams. And thus we have reached this rather summary distinction which must nevertheless clarify our inquiry. The night dreamer cannot articulate a *cogito*. The night dream is a dream without a dreamer. On the contrary, the dreamer of reverie remains conscious enough to say: it is I who dream the reverie, it is I who am content to dream my reverie, happy with this leisure in which I no longer have the task of thinking. That is what we have tried to show with the help of poets' reveries in the chapter entitled "The *Cogito* of the Dreamer."

But the dreamer of reveries does not abstract himself in the solitude of a *cogito*. His dreaming *cogito* has, as philosophers say, its *cogitatum* immediately. Immediately, reverie has a simple object, the friend and companion of the dreamer. Naturally, we have borrowed from poets our examples of objects poetized by reverie. In living off all the reflecting light furnished by poets, the I which dreams the reverie reveals itself not as poet but as poetizing I.

After this excursion into hardened philosophy, we return in one last chapter to an examination of the extreme images of reverie which are ceaselessly attempted in the dialectic between the excited subject and the excessive world. Here I have tried to follow the images which open up or enlarge the world. Cosmic images are sometimes so majestic that philosophers take them for thoughts. By doing our best to relive them, we have tried to show that they are relaxations of reverie. Reverie helps us inhabit the world, inhabit the happiness of the world. So we have taken "Reverie and Cosmos" as the title of this chapter. It will be understood that such a vast problem cannot be treated in a short chapter. We have touched on it many times in the course of earlier research on imagination without ever treating it fully. We would be happy today if we could, at least, pose the problem a little more clearly. Imagined worlds determine profound communions of reveries. The point can be reached where one can interrogate a heart by asking it to confess its enthusiasms inspired by the grandeur of the contemplated world, the world imagined in deep contemplation. How certainly would the psychoanalysts, those masters of indirect interrogation, find new keys for getting to the bottom of a soul if they practiced a little cosmo-analysis! Here is an example of cosmo-analysis taken from a passage by Fromentin. In the decisive moments of his passion, Dominique leads Madeleine to sites he had chosen with great care:

Above all, I liked to try out on Madeleine the effect of certain influences which are physical rather than moral and to which I myself was so continually subjected. I would confront her with certain landscape paintings chosen from among those which, invariably composed of a little greenery, a great deal of sun and an immense expanse of sea, had the infallible gift for moving me. I would observe in what sense she would be struck by them, in what respects of indigence or grandeur this sad, grave and always barren landscape could please her. As much as I could, I would interrogate her on these details of wholly exterior sensitivity.[15]

Thus, confronted with an immensity, the person who is being interrogated seems to be naturally sincere. The site overwhelms poor and fluid social "situations." What great value, then, an album of sites would have for interrogating our solitary being and revealing the world where we must live in order to be ourselves! We receive this album of sites from reverie with a prodigality that we would not find in many voyages. We imagine worlds where our life would take on all its brilliance, warmth and development. Poets lead us into cosmoses which are being endlessly renewed. During the Romantic period, the landscape was a tool of sentimentality. So in the last chapter of this book, we have tried to study the expansion of being which we receive from cosmic reveries. With reveries of cosmos, the dreamer knows reverie without responsibility, reverie which does not ask for proof. At the end, imagining a cosmos is the most natural destiny of reverie.

---

[15] *Dominque*, p. 179.

VII

At the conclusion of this Introduction, let us state briefly where, in our solitude and without possible recourse to psychological inquiries, we must look for our documentation. It comes from books; reading is our whole life.

Reading is a *dimension* of the modern psychism, a dimension which transposes psychic phenomena already transposed by writing. Written language must be considered as a particular psychic reality. The book is permanent; it is an object in your field of vision. It speaks to you with a monotonous authority which even its author would not have. You are fairly obliged to read what is written. Besides, in writing, the author has already performed a transposition. He would not *say* what he has written. He has entered—his protests are in vain here—the realm of the written psychism.

Here, the educated psychism takes on its permanence. How profound is Edgar Quinet's passage where he speaks of the force of transmission in the Ramayana.[16] Valmiki says to his disciples:

Learn the revealed poem; it gives virtue and wealth: full of sweetness when it is adapted to the three measures of time, sweeter still if it is married to the sound of instruments or if it is sung on the seven cords of the voice. The delighted ear excites love, courage, anguish, terror. . . . O the great poem, the faithful image of truth.

Slow and mute reading gives the ear all these concerts.

But the best proof of the specificity of the book is that it is at once a reality of the virtual and a virtuality of the real. Reading a novel, we are placed in another life where we suffer, hope and sympathize, but just the same with the complex impression that our anguish remains under the domination of our liberty, that our anguish is not radical. Any anguishing book can, therefore, provide a technique for the reduction of anguish. An anguishing book offers anguished people a homeopathy of anguish. But this homeopathy works above all during a meditative reading, one which is stabilized by literary interest. Then two levels of the

---

16 Edgar Quinet, *Le génie des religions. L'épopée indienne*, p. 143.

psychism separate, the reader participates at the two levels, and when he becomes quite conscious of the *aesthetics of anguish,* he is quite close to discovering facticity. For anguish is factitious: we are made to breathe easy.

And it is in that way that poetry—summit of all aesthetic joy— is beneficial.

Without the help of poets, what can a philosopher, weighted down with years, do if he persists in talking about the imagination? He has no one to test. He would immediately get lost in the labyrinth of tests and counter-tests, where the subject being examined by the psychologist struggles. Besides, do there really exist in the psychologist's arsenal tests of the imagination? Are there psychologists exalted enough to be constantly renewing the objective techniques for a study of the exalted imagination? Poets will always imagine faster than those who watch them imagining.

How can we enter the poetisphere of our time? An era of free imagination has just begun. From everywhere, images invade the air, go from one world to another, and call both ears and eyes to enlarged dreams. Poets abound, the great and the small, the famous and the obscure, those who love and those who dazzle. Whoever lives for poetry must read everything. How often has the light of a new idea sprung for me from a simple brochure! When one allows himself to be animated by new images, he discovers iridescence in the images of old books. Poetic ages unite in a living memory. The new age awakens the old. The old age comes to live again in the new. Poetry is never as unified as when it diversifies.

What benefits new books bring us! I would like a basket full of books telling the youth of images which fall from heaven for me every day. This desire is natural. This prodigy is easy. For, up there, in heaven, isn't paradise an immense library?

But it is not sufficient to receive; one must welcome. One must, say the pedagogue and the dietician in the same voice, "assimilate." In order to do that, we are advised not to read too fast and to be careful not to swallow too large a bite. We are told to divide each difficulty into as many parts as possible, the better to solve them. Yes, chew well, drink a little at a time, savor poems line by line. All these precepts are well and good. But one precept orders them. One first needs a good desire to eat, drink and read. One must want to read a lot, read more, always read.

Thus, in the morning, before the books piled high on my table, to the god of reading, I say my prayer of the devouring reader: "Give us this day our daily hunger . . ."

One

Reveries on Reverie
(The Word Dreamer)

At the bottom of each word
I'm a spectator at my birth.
  Alain Bosquet,
  Premier poème.

I have my amulets: words.
  Henri Bosco,
  Sites et paysages

I

Dreams (*rêve*, m.) and reveries (*rêverie*, f.), dreams (*songe*, m.) and daydreams (*songerie*, f.), memories (*souvenir*, m.) and remembrance (*souvenance*, f.) are all indications of a need to make everything feminine which is enveloping and soft above and beyond the too simply masculine designations for our states of mind. That is, without a doubt, a very insignificant remark in the eyes of philosophers who speak the language of the universal, a very insignificant remark in the eyes of thinkers who hold language to be a simple instrument which must be forced to express all the subtleties of thought with precision. But how would a dreaming (*songeur*) philosopher who ceases to reflect when he is imagining and who has thus admitted to himself the divorce between intellect and imagination, how could such a philosopher, when he dreams about language and when words are coming out of the very depths of dreams (*songe*) for him, not be sensitive to the rivalry between the masculine and the feminine which he discovers at the origin of speech? Already, by the gender of the words that designate them, dream (*rêve*) and reverie appear to be different. Nuances are lost when one considers dream and reverie as two varieties of the same oneiric phenomenon. Rather let us keep the clarity which is the genius of our language. Let us get to the bottom of nuance and try to realize the femininity of reverie.

Roughly speaking—and I shall try to suggest this to the willing reader—the dream (*rêve*) is masculine; reverie is feminine. Then, by using the division of the psyche into *animus* and *anima,* as this division has been established by the psychology of the depths, we shall show that reverie is, as much in man as in woman, a manifestation of the *anima.* But first, through a reverie on the words themselves, we must prepare the intimate convictions which assure the permanence of femininity in every human psyche.

II

In order to close in on the nucleus of feminine reverie, we shall rely on the feminine element of words.

"Orbs of words, murmuring memory," [1] says the poet.

By dreaming on our mother tongue, in our mother tongue— can one live reveries in a tongue other than the one committed to the "murmuring memory?"—we believe we can recognize a preference for reverie in feminine words. Feminine desinences already have a certain softness. But the antepenultimate is also penetrated by this softness. There are words in which the feminine element impregnates every syllable. Such words are *reverie words.* They belong to the language of the *anima.*

But since I am at the threshold of a book where phenomenological sincerity is a method, I ought to say that, while under the impression that I was thinking, I have often daydreamed (*rêvasser*) on the masculine or feminine gender of moral qualities like pride (*orgueil,* m.) and vanity (*vanité,* f.), courage (*courage,* m.) and passion (*passion,* f.). It seemed to me that the masculine and feminine elements in these words accentuated the contrasts, dramatized moral life. Then from among the ideas where I was wandering, I would pass to the names of things where I was sure to dream well. I used to like knowing that in French the names of rivers are generally feminine. It is so natural! The Aube and the Seine, the Moselle and the Loire are my only rivers. The Rhone (m.) and the Rhine (m.) are, to my way of thinking, linguistic monsters. They carry down water from the glaciers. Aren't feminine names necessary if we wish to respect the femininity of real water (*eau,* f.)?

That is only my first example of word reveries. For, when I was

---

1 Henri Capien, *Signes.* Seghers, 1955.

fortunate enough to have a dictionary, I would let myself be enchanted for hours on end by the feminine of words. My reverie would follow the inflections of softness. The feminine element in a word accentuates the joy of speaking. But for that one needs a certain love of slow sonorities.

This is not always as easy as one thinks. Some things are so solid in their reality that one forgets to dream upon their name. Not very long ago, I discovered that the chimney (*cheminée,* f.) was a path (*chemin,* m.), the path of soft smoke (*fumée,* f.) which wends its way (*cheminer*) slowly toward the sky.

Sometimes the grammatical act which gives a feminine to a being glorified in the masculine is pure clumsiness. The centaur is, of course, the prestigious ideal of a horseman who knows full well that he will never be unseated. But what might the centauress be? Who can dream of the centauress? It was very much later that my word reverie found its balance. While dreaming as I read the botanical dictionary called *Botannique chrétienne* by the Abbé Migne, I discovered that the dreamer's feminine of the word *centaure* was the *centaurée.* It is, of course, a small flower, but its power is great, truly worthy of the medical knowledge of Chiron, the superhuman centaur. Doesn't Pliny tell us that the *centaurée* cures torn flesh? Boil up the *centaurée* with some pieces of meat, and they will come back together in their primitive unity. Beautiful words are already remedies.[2]

When I hesitate to confide such reveries which, however, often come back to mind, I take courage in reading Nodier. Nodier used to dream so often between words and things and was completely happy to be giving names. "There is something marvelously soft in the study of nature which attaches a name to every being, a thought to every name, affection and memories to every thought."[3] One more subtlety in uniting the name and the thing with this affection for well-named things stimulates waves of femininity within us. To love things for their use is a function of the

---

[2] The word "centauress" must be pardoned because Rimbaud could see "the heights where seraphic centauresses evolve among the avalanches" (*Les illuminations,* "Villes"). It is essential, however, to refrain from imagining them galloping across the plains.

[3] Charles Nodier, *Souvenirs de jeunesse,* p. 18.

masculine. They are components (*pièces*) of our actions, of our live actions. But to love them intimately, for themselves, with the slownesses of the feminine, that is what leads us into the labyrinth of the intimate Nature of things. Thus, in "feminine reveries," I complete the very captivating text where Nodier unites his double love of words and things, his double love of the grammarian and the botanist.

Naturally, a simple grammatical desinence, a random mute *e* attached to a noun which has a masculine career has never been sufficient, in my dictionary meditation, to provide me with the great dreams (*songes*) of femininity. I had to feel the word feminized throughout and endowed with an irrevocable feminine element.

How disturbing then, when in passing from one language to another, one experiences a femininity being lost or masked by masculine sounds! C. G. Jung points out "that in Latin, names of trees have masculine endings and yet are feminine." [4] This lack of agreement between sounds and genders explains to a certain extent the numerous androgynous images associated with the substance of trees. In such cases, the substance contradicts the substantive. Hermaphroditism and Amphibology intermingle. They end up supporting each other in the reveries of a word dreamer. One begins to make a mistake while speaking and he finishes by enjoying the union of opposites. Proudhon who rarely dreams and quickly becomes scholarly immediately finds a cause for the feminine of Latin names of trees: "It is doubtless," he says, "because of the fructification." [5] But Proudhon does not give us enough reveries to help us pass from the apple (*pomme,* f.) to the apple tree (*pommier,* m.) and make the feminine element of the apple flow all the way back to the tree.

In going from one language to another, what a lot of scandals we must occasionally pass through in order to accept improbable femininities which disturb the most natural reveries! Numerous cosmic texts in German where the sun and moon intervene seem to me personally impossible to dream because of the extraordi-

---

4 C. G. Jung, *Métamorphoses de l'âme,* translation, p. 371.
5 Proudhon, *Un essai de grammaire générale.* In the appendix to Bergier's book, *Les éléments primitifs des langues* (Besançon and Paris, 1850), p. 266.

nary inversion which gives the sun (*soleil,* m.) the feminine gender and the moon (*lune,* f.) the masculine gender. When grammatical discipline obliges adjectives to become masculine in order to associate themselves with the moon, a French dreamer has the impression that his lunar reverie is being perverted.

On the other hand, from one language to another, what a beautiful moment of reading when one conquers a feminine! A conquered feminine can deepen an entire poem. Thus, in a piece of Heinrich Heine's poetry, the poet tells the dream (*rêve*) of an isolated spruce slumbering under the ice and snow, lost in solitude upon an arid northern plain: "The spruce dreams (*rêve*) of a palm tree which, way off in the distant Orient, grieves, solitary and taciturn upon the slope of a burning rock." [6] Spruce of the North, palm tree of the South, icy solitude, burning solitude: a French reader must dream upon these antitheses (both *palmier* and *sapin* are masculine in French). How many more reveries are open to the German reader since in German the word "spruce" is masculine while the word for palm tree is feminine! Then in the straight and vigorous tree beneath the ice, what a lot of dreams are directed toward the feminine tree, open in every one of its palms, attentive to every breeze! As for me, I have infinite dreams (*rêves*) by putting this being which is the palm tree in the feminine. Seeing so much greenery, such an exuberance of green palms emerging from the scaly corset of a rude trunk, I take this beautiful being of the South to be the vegetable siren, the siren of the sands.

As green makes red "sing" in a painting, a feminine word in poetry can bring grace to the masculine being. In Renée Mauperin's garden a horticulturist, such as one could only encounter in an imaginary life, made rose bushes climb the entire length of a spruce. The old tree can thus "wave roses in its green arms." [7] Who will ever tell us of the marriage of the spruce (*sapin,* m.) and the rose (*rose,* f.)? I am grateful to novelists so sharply in tune with human passions that they had the kindness to put roses in the arms of the cold tree.

---

[6] Quoted by Albert Béguin, *L'âme romantique et le rêve,* 1st edition, vol. II, p. 313.
[7] Edmond and Jules de Goncourt, *Renée Mauperin* (Paris, 1879), p. 101.

When, in passing from one language to another, inversions affect beings of one of our congenital oneirisms, we feel our poetic aspirations greatly divided. It would be nice to dream a great object of reveries twice when it is presented in a new "gender."

At Nuremberg, in front of the "venerable Fountain of the Virtues," Johannes Joergensen exclaims: "Your name seems so beautiful to me! The word 'fountain' contains within it a poetry which has always moved me very deeply, above all in the German form *Brunnen* whose consonance seems to prolong within me a soft impression of repose." [8] To appreciate the speech delights experienced by the Danish writer, it would be a good idea to know what the gender of the word "fountain" is in his mother tongue. But already for us as a French reader Joergensen's passage upsets and disturbs radical reveries. Is it possible that there are languages which put the fountain in the masculine? All of a sudden the *Brunnen* (m.) provides me with diabolical reveries as if the world had just changed its nature. By dreaming a little more, in a different way, *le Brunnen* finally speaks to me. I distinctly hear the *Brunnen* making a deeper sound than the fountain (*fontaine,* f.). It spills over less gently than the fountains in my country. Brunnen-Fountain are two original sounds for a pure, fresh water. And yet for the person who likes to speak while dreaming his words, the same water does not come from the fountain and the *Brunnen*. The difference of gender overturns all my reveries. It is really the entire reverie which changes *gender*. But going off to dream in a language other than the mother tongue is doubtless a grave temptation. I must be faithful to my fountain.

Concerning the reversals of masculine and feminine values in passing from one language to another, linguists would certainly furnish many explanations for such anomalies. I would certainly have profited from letting the grammarians instruct me. Yet let us just mention our astonishment at seeing so many linguists dispose of the problem by saying that the masculine or feminine of nouns results from chance. Obviously, one does not find any reason for

---

[8] Johannes Joergensen, *Le Livre de route,* translated by Teodor de Wyzewa (Paris, 1916), p. 12.

the situation if he limits himself precisely to reasonable reasons. Perhaps an oneiric examination would be necessary. Simone de Beauvoir seems disappointed by the lack of curiosity on the part of erudite philology. She writes: "On this question of the gender of words, philology is rather mysterious; all linguists agree in recognizing that the distribution of concrete words into genders is purely accidental. Yet in French most of the entities belong to the feminine: beauty, loyalty, etc." [9] The "etc." shortens the proof a bit. But an important theme of the femininity of words is indicated in this text. The woman is the ideal of human nature and "the ideal which man posits opposite himself as the essential Other; he feminizes it because the woman is the palpable figure of otherness (*altérité*); that is why nearly all allegories, in language, as in iconography, are women."

Words, in our scholarly cultures, have so often been defined, redefined and pigeonholed with so much precision in our dictionaries that they have truly become instruments of thought. They have lost their power for internal oneirism. In order to return to this oneirism which is related to nouns, it would be necessary to make an inquiry into nouns which still dream, nouns which are "children of the night." Indeed, when Clémence Ramnoux is studying the philosophy of Heraclitus, she conducts her inquiry as the subtitle of her book indicates: *by looking for "the man between things and words."* [10] And the words for great things like night (*nuit*, f.) and day (*jour*, m.), like sleep (*sommeil*, m.) death (*mort*, f.), like sky (*ciel*, m.) and earth (*terre*, f.) take on their meaning only by designating themselves as "couples." One couple dominates another couple; one couple engenders another couple. Any cosmology is a spoken cosmology. By making gods out of them, you upset the meaning. But seen more closely, as by modern historians like Clémence Ramnoux, the problem does not simplify as quickly. In fact, as soon as a worldly being has any force (*puissance*), it is very close to classifying itself either as a masculine or feminine force. Every force has a sex; it can even be

9 Simone de Beauvoir, *Le deuxième sexe*, Gallimard, vol. I, p. 286, text and note.
10 Clémence Ramnoux, *Héraclite ou l'homme entre les choses et les mots* (Paris, 1959) Les Belles Lettres.

bisexual. Never will it be neuter; at least, it will not remain neuter very long. When a cosmological trinity is set up, it must be designated as 1 + 2 like the chaos from which emerge the Erebos and the Nyx.

With meanings which evolve from the human to the divine, from tangible facts to dreams (*songes*), words take on a certain thickness of meaning.

But from the moment it is understood that every force is accompanied by a harmonics of sexuality, it becomes natural to examine (*ausculter*) the weighted words, those words which have a force (*puissance*). In our life as a civilized person in the industrial age, we are invaded by objects; how could an object have a "force" when it no longer has individuality? But let us go a little way toward the distant past of objects. Let us put our reveries back in front of a familiar object. Then let us dream further yet, so far even that we lose ourselves in our reveries when we want to know how an object might have found its name. By dreaming between thing and word in the modesty of familiar things, as Clémence Ramnoux, in the Heraclitian shadows, does for the grandeurs of human destiny, the object, the modest object emerges to play its role in the world, in a word which dreams little as well as big. Reverie sacralizes its object. From the beloved familiar object to the sacred personal object it is only a step. Soon the object is an amulet which helps us and protects us in life. Its help is maternal or paternal. Every amulet has a sex. The name of an amulet does not have the right to be in the wrong gender.

At any rate, for lack of education in the problems of linguistics, we are not pretending to educate the reader in this leisurely book. It is not by starting from *knowledge* (*savoir*) that one can really dream, dream without restraint, dream in an uncensored reverie. I have no other goal in this present chapter than to present a "case"—my personal case—the case of a word dreamer.

III

But would linguistic explanations really deepen our reverie? Our reverie will always be stimulated more by a singular and even adventurous hypothesis than by a scholarly demonstration. How can one help but be amused by the double imperialism which Bernardin de Saint-Pierre accords to appellation? Didn't this great dreamer say, "It would be quite curious to investigate whether masculine names have been given by women and feminine names by men to things which serve more particularly the usages of each sex and if the first were made *masculine* because they present characteristics of force and power and the second *feminine* because they present characteristics of grace and pleasure?" Bescherelle, who quotes Bernardin de Saint-Pierre without reference in his dictionary under the article *gender,* remains a tranquil lexicographer on this problem. He disposes of the problem, like so many others, by saying that for inanimate objects, the designation as masculine or feminine is arbitrary. But is it so simple, when one is dreaming, to say where the realm of the animate ends?

And if it is the animate which commands, isn't it necessary to put the most animated of all beings first, the man and the woman who are both going to be principles of personalization? For Schelling, every opposition has been translated more or less naturally into an opposition between the masculine and the feminine. "Isn't every appellation already a personification? And in light of the fact that every language designates the objects embodying an *opposition* by differences of gender, and given that we say, for example, sky and earth (*le ciel et la terre*) . . . aren't we thus singularly close to expressing spiritual notions by masculine and feminine divinities?" This text appears in the *Introduction to the Philosophy of Mythology.*[11] It indicates to us the long destiny of the opposition of genders which proceeds from things to divinities by way of man. And thus it is that Schelling can add: "One is almost tempted to say that the language itself is a mythology deprived of its vitality, a bloodless mythology so to speak, which has only preserved in a formal and abstract form what mythology contains in living and concrete form." That so great a philosopher goes so far perhaps justifies a word dreamer who, in his reverie, returns a little "vitality" to the faded oppositions.

For Proudhon,[12] ". . . in every species of animal, the female is

---

[11] F. W. Schelling, *Introduction à la philosophie de la mythologie.* Translated by S. Jankélévitch (Aubier, 1945), vol. I, p. 62.
[12] *Loc. cit.,* p. 265.

ordinarily the smallest, weakest and most delicate being: it was natural to designate this sex by the attribute which characterizes it; and to this effect the name lengthens into a particular ending which is the image of softness, weakness, and smallness. It was a description by analogy, and at first, the feminine constituted among nouns what we call the *diminutive*. In every language, then, the feminine ending was softer, more tender one might say, than that of the masculine."

This reference to the *diminutive* leaves many dreams (*songes*) in suspense. Proudhon apparently did not dream of the beauty of things becoming small. But his mention of a tender vocality attached to feminine words cannot help but echo in the reveries of a word dreamer.[13]

But the last word has not been spoken by employing codified syllables. Sometimes, in order to express all the psychological subtleties, a great writer manages to create or set up "doublets" on the theme of genders and put a suitable masculine and feminine together in the right place. For example, when will-o'-the-wisps—beings of very indeterminate sex—are to seduce men or women, they become precisely, according to the person to be led astray, *flambettes* (f.) or *flamboires* (m.).[14]

> Look out for the *flamboires,* little girl!
> Look out for the *flambettes,* booby!

How appropriate this warning is for the person who knows how to love words with the necessary passion.

And in the sinister mode, to frighten a man or a woman still more, black crows (*corbeaux,* m.) become "fat *coares* (f.)." [15]

Everything which is conflict or attraction in the human psychism is accentuated and given precision when the nuances which make words masculine or feminine are added to the most tenuous of contradictions and the most confused of communions. Hence,

---

13 But what a drama in a family of words when the masculine is smaller than the feminine, when the pitcher (*cruche,* f.) is bigger than the little jug (*cruchon,* m.)!
14 Cf. George Sand, *Légendes rustiques,* p. 133.
15 George Sand, *loc. cit.,* p. 147.

how "mutilated" those languages must be which have lost the original truths of gender through an aging of their grammar! And what a great service one is done by French—a passionate language which has not wanted to preserve a "neuter" gender, that gender which does not choose when it is so agreeable to multiply the occasions for choosing!

But let us give an example of this pleasure of choosing, this pleasure of associating the masculine and the feminine. A word reverie adds an indescribable spice to the poetic reverie. It seems to us that stylistics would do well to add to its various methods of examination a fairly systematic inquiry into the relative abundance of masculine and feminine words. But in this area, a statistic would not be sufficient. The "weight" must be determined, the tonality of preferences measured. To prepare oneself for these sentimental measurements of an author's vocabulary, it would perhaps be necessary—I blush to give this advice—to allow oneself to become, in some good moments of repose, a word dreamer.

But if I hesitate over the method, I have more confidence in examples lived out by poets.

IV

First, here is a model of the union between the masculine of a word and the feminine.

Because he is a poet, the good padre Jean Perrin dreams "Of marrying the dawn with the light of the moon." [*De marier l'aurore* (f.) *avec le clair de lune.*] [16] That is a wish which will never be on the lips of an Anglican pastor condemned to dream in a language without genders. All the bells of the bindweed in the parish of Faremoutiers, whether they are hanging on the hedge or in the bushes, ring a full peal for this marriage of words celebrated by the poet.

Another example will be much different. It will tell of the royalty of the feminine in objects. We shall take it from a tale by Rachilde. It is a tale of youth. She must have written it at the time she was writing Monsieur Vénus. In this story, Rachilde sets

---

[16] Jean Perrin, *La colline d'ivoire*, p. 28.

out to describe the onrush of flowers going to cure the Tuscan plain ravaged by the plague.[17] Here, the rose is the energetic, conquering, dominating feminine: "The roses, mouths of glowing embers, flames of flesh (licked) at the incorruptibility of the marble." Other roses of a "clinging species" invade the bell tower. Projecting "the forest of their ferocious briars through an ogive," it "attached itself—this clinging species—to the entire length of a cord and made it waver under the weight of its young buds." And when there were a hundred of them pulling on the cord, the alarm bell rang. "The roses were ringing the alarm bell. The furnace of their passionate odor was added to the fire of the amorous sky." Then "the army of flowers answers the call of its queen" so that floral life may triumph over accursed life. The plants with male names follow the general surge at a less ardent pace: "Honeysuckles with digited pistils advanced as if on clawed hands . . . The couch grass, lycopods, mignonettes, green and gray plebeians . . . multiplied in immense carpets over which ran the avant-garde of mad bindweed bearing cups from which trickled a blue drunkenness." [18]

Thus, in such a text, masculine and feminine nouns are well sorted out and neatly set in opposition. One could easily find other proofs by pursuing the gender analysis, as we have outlined it, from one end of Rachilde's story to the other.

From a rose (*rose*, f.) which licks at marble (*marbre*, m.) psychoanalysts could easily compose a case history. But by assigning too distant psychological responsibilities to the page of poetry, they deprive us of the joy of speaking. They take the words out of our mouths. The analysis of a literary passage by the gender of the words—genosanalysis—is based on values which will appear superficial to psychologists, psychoanalysts and thinkers. But to us, it appears as one line of inquiry—there are many others!—for ordering the simple joys of speech.

At any rate, let us deposit Rachilde's passage in the dossier on

[17] Rachilde, *Contes et nouvelles* . . . Mercure de France, 1900, pp. 54–55. The story is entitled "Le Mortis." It is dedicated to Alfred Jarry whom Rachilde will later call the super-male of letters (cf. *Jarry, ou le Surmâle de lettres,* Grasset, 1928).
[18] Rachilde, *loc. cit.*, p. 56.

the super-feminine. And to avoid all confusion, let us recall that, in 1927, Rachilde published a book entitled *Why I am not a Feminist*.

Finally, let us add, with the support of examples like those we are citing, that passages strongly marked by a privileged grammatical gender or carefully balanced between the masculine and feminine genders lose part of their "charm" if translated into an asexual language. We are repeating this remark in relation to a very characteristic text. But it never leaves our mind. It will always be a polemical argument to give us confidence in our reading dreams (*songes*).

So let us read as a devourer of texts which feed our mania.

Without reverberating to the feminine of the nouns "prairie" (*prarie*, f.) and "dawn" (*aube*, f.), how can one adequately experience this memory of an adolescent who is waiting for someone to love him: "Having made her appearance in the blond prairie, the dawn courted the stout prudish poppies (*coquelicot*, m.)." [19]

Coquelicot is one of the rare flowers in the masculine, one which does not keep its petals very well, that the least little thing defoliates, that defends only feebly the masculine red of its name.

But words, the words with their own temperament are already "courting," and it is thus that, through the voice of the poet, the blond dawn teases the red poppy.

In other texts by Saint-George-de-Bouhélier, the loves of the dawn and the poppy are less gentle, and one might even say, less preliminary: "The dawn (*aurore*, f.) is rumbling in the thunder of the poppies." [20] As for the poet's love, the gentle Clarisse, "poppies that were too big gave her a fright." [21] The day arrives when in passing from childhood to a more virile age, the poet can write: "I gather enormous poppies without going up in flames at their contact." [22] The masculine fire of the poppies has ceased being "prudish." There are thus flowers which accompany us throughout life, changing a little in nature as the poems change.

---

[19] Saint-Georges-de-Bouhélier, *L'hiver en méditation*, Mercure de France, 1896, p. 46.
[20] *Loc. cit.*, p. 47.
[21] *Loc. cit.*, p. 29.
[22] *Loc. cit.*, p. 53.

Where are the rustic virtues of the poppies of yesteryear? For a word dreamer, the word *coquelicot* lends itself to laughter. It sounds too noisy. It is difficult for such a word to be the germ of an agreeably pursued reverie. The word dreamer would be very clever indeed if he were to find a feminine counterpart for the poppy which would set the reverie in motion. The daisy (*marguerite*, f.)—another apoetic word—would not help at all. More genius is needed to make literary bouquets.

We shall have more pleasure dreaming the bouquets which Félix prepares for Mme de Mortsauf in *The Lily in the Valley*. As Balzac wrote them, they are, besides being bouquets of flowers, bouquets of words, even bouquets of syllables. A genosanalyst hears them in the correct balance of masculine and feminine words. Here are "Bengal roses strewn among the mad lace of the wild carrot, the feathers of the cotton grass, the marabou feathers of goat's beard, the umbellets of wild chervil, the dainty St. Andrews' crosses of milkwhite crosswort, the corymbs of yarrow . . ." [23] Masculine ornaments come to feminine flowers and vice versa. One cannot get away from the idea that the author wanted this balance. Perhaps the field botanist *sees* such *literary* bouquets but a reader as sensitized as Balzac was to masculine and feminine words, *hears* them. Entire pages are filled with *vocal flowers:* "Around the flaired neck of the porcelain vase, imagine a wide border composed entirely of the white tufts peculiar to the stone crop of the grape vines in Touraine, a vague image of the desired forms, rolled like those of an obedient woman slave. From this foundation emerge the spirals of the white-belled bindweed, sprigs of rose-colored commack mixed with a few ferns and some young oak saplings with magnificently colorful and lustrous leaves; they all come forward humbly prostrate like weeping willows, as timid and as pleading as prayers." [24]

---

23 Balzac, *Le lys dans la vallée*, p. 125. ". . . *les roses (f.) du Bengale clairsemées parmi les folles dentelles (f.) du daucus (m.) les plumes (f.) de la linaigrette (f.), les marabouts (m.) de la reine des prés (f.) les ombellules (f.) du cerfeuil (m.) sauvage, les mignons sautoirs (m.) de la croisette (f.) au blanc de lait (m.), les corymbes (m.) de mille-feuilles (f.) . . ."*
24 "*Autour du col (m.) évasé de la porcelaine (f.), supposez une forte marge uniquement composée des touffes (f.) particulières au sédum (m.) des vignes (f.) en Touraine, vague image des formes souhaitées, roulées comme*

A psychologist who believed in words would perhaps penetrate the sentimental composition of such bouquets. In them, each flower is a confession, discreet or glaring, premeditated or involuntary. Sometimes a flower tells of a revolt, sometimes of a submission, an unhappiness or a hope. And what a participation in written love it would be if we, the simple reader, were to imagine ourselves at the novelist's worktable. Didn't Balzac himself say that all the floral decorations of his pages were "flowers of the writing desk?" [25] In those passages where the novel stops while the bouquets gather, Balzac is a word dreamer. The bouquets of flowers are bouquets of names of flowers.

When it happens that feminine words are lacking in a passage, the style takes on a massive character, inclining toward the abstract. A poet's ear is not mistaken. Thus, Claudel denounces the monotony of a celibate harmony in Flaubert: "Masculine endings dominate, terminating each cadence with a hard, dull thud lacking elasticity and echo. The fault of French which is that of coming from an accelerated movement to fall head first at the last syllable is not alleviated here by any artifice. The author seems to be unaware of the balloon of the feminines, the great wings of the parenthetical clause which, far from weighing down the sentence, lightens it and lets it touch down to earth only when all its meaning has been exhausted." [26] And in a note which should attract the attention of the stylisticians, Claudel shows how a sentence can vibrate with the interjection of a feminine parenthetical clause:

Let us suppose, he says, that Pascal had written: *Man is only a reed;* the voice finds no sure support, and the mind remains in painful suspense, but he wrote:

L'homme n'est qu'un roseau, *le plus faible de la Nature,* mais c'est un roseau pensant

---

celles d'une esclave soumise. De cette assise sortent les spirales (f.) des liserons (m.) à cloches (f.) blanches, les brindilles (f.) de la bugrane rose, mêlées de quelques fougères (f.), de quelques jeunes pousses de chêne (m.) aux feuilles (f.) magnifiquement colorées et lustrées; toutes s'avancent prosternées humblement comme des saules pleureurs (m.) timides et suppliantes comme des prières (f.)."

[25] *Loc. cit.,* p. 121.
[26] Paul Claudel, *Positions et propositions,* Mercure de France, vol. 1, p. 78.

—and the sentence vibrates throughout with a magnificent full-ness.

In another note (p. 79) Claudel adds: "It would be unfair to forget that sometimes Flaubert has managed certain moderate successes. For example: 'and I, upon the last branch, I lit up the summer nights with my face.' " [27]

V

When one devotes himself with predilection to such word reveries, it is very comforting to come across a brother-in-fancy in his reading. Not very long ago, I was reading the work of a poet who, at the prime of life, is more audacious than I. When a great word takes to dreaming in its own substance, he wants to put it in the feminine, contrary to ordinary practice. Edmond Gilliard dreams first of all of feeling the word "silence" (*silence*, m.) in its essential femininity. For him the quality of silence is "entirely feminine; it must let all speech penetrate it to the very substance of the Word . . . I have difficulty," says the poet, "in maintaining, in front of the word 'silence,' the article which defines it grammatically as masculine." [28]

Perhaps the word "silence" has been given masculine hardness because it is given the imperative mode. "Silence," says the master who wants to be listened to passively. But when silence brings peace into a solitary soul, one clearly feels that the silence is preparing the atmosphere for a tranquil *anima*.

Here psychological examination is offended by proofs taken from everyday life. It is only too easy to characterize silence as a withdrawal full of hostility, rancor and sulkiness. The poet solicits us to dream well beyond those psychological conflicts which fragment people who do not know how to dream.

---

[27] The grammarian F. Burggraff ended his chapter on genders with a remark on the euphony of a double-gender language in the following terms: "The diversity of endings with which genders are marked, notes Court de Gebelin, spreads a great harmony throughout the discourse; it banishes uniformity and monotony from it; for these endings, some being strong, some gentle, there results a mixture of gentle sounds and sounds full of force which gives it much charm." (F. Burggraff, *Principes de grammaire générale ou exposition raisonée des éléments du langage*, Liège, 1863, p. 230).

[28] Edmond Gilliard, *Hymne terrestre*. Seghers, 1958, pp. 97–98.

It is quite evident that a barrier must be cleared in order to escape the psychologists and enter into a realm which is not "auto-observant," where we ourselves no longer divide ourselves into observer and observed. Then the dreamer is completely dissolved (*fondu*) in his reverie. His reverie is his silent life. It is that silent peace which the poet wants to convey to us.

Happy is the man who knows or even the man who remembers those silent vigils where silence itself was the sign of the communion of souls!

With what tenderness Francis Jammes, remembering such times, could write: "I would tell you to be still when you were saying nothing." Then opens the reverie without plans, without a past, entirely given over to the presence of the communion of souls in the silence and peace of the feminine.

Following silence, it is space that Edmond Gilliard has enveloped in a feminine reverie: "My pen stumbles," he says, "on the article which strangles access to the accepting expanse. The masculine inversion of space is an insult to its fecundity. Being of the nature of space, my silence is feminine."

In upsetting the routines of grammar twice, Edmond Gilliard finds the double femininity of silence and space (both masculine in French), one sustaining the other.

In order to grasp silence better yet in the lairs of femininity, the poet wants space to be a goatskin bottle (*outre*, f.). He cocks his ear at the opening of the wineskin so that the silence will make him hear the murmurings of the feminine. He writes: "My 'Wineskin' is a great opening for eavesdropping." In such eavesdropping, voices are going *to be born,* born from the entirely feminine fecundity of silence and space, from the quiet peace of expanse.

The title of Edmond Gilliard's poetic meditation is a triumph of the feminine—*Revenance* (f.) *de l'Outre.*[29]

The psychoanalyst will not take long to put his label "return

---

[29] Does it grate on the ear when a great writer puts *outre* in the masculine? Doesn't Voltaire say: "Master, one does not eat my basilic; I have put it in a small wineskin (*petit outre*, m.) well inflated and covered with a fine pelt." Quoted by M. P. Poitevin, *La grammaire, les écrivains et les typographes modernes. Cacographie et cacologie historiques,* p. 19.

to the womb" upon such a poem. But the gentle work of words is not explained by a determination that general. If it were simply a question of a "return to the womb," how would we explain a reverie which wants to transform the mother tongue? Or again how can such distant impulsions coming from an attachment to the mother be so constructive in the poetic language?

The psychology of the faraway must not overload the psychology of the present being, the being present in its language, living in its language. However distant the source, poetic reveries are also born from the living forces of language. The expression reacts strongly on the sentiments expressed. By being satisfied to answer only "return to the womb" to enigmas which are being multiplied as they are being expressed, the psychoanalyst does not help us live the life of language, a spoken life which is lived in nuance, by nuance. It is necessary to dream more, dream in the very life of the language in order to feel how, to borrow Proudhon's expression, man could "give sexes to his words." [30]

VI

In an old article reprinted in the *Carré rouge*,[31] Edmond Gilliard tells of his joys and sorrows as an artisan of language: "If I were surer of my craft," he writes, "how proudly I would put out my sign: 'Words cleaned here . . .' Word scraper, bootblack for vocables: a hard, but useful trade."

As for me, in the happy mornings when I am being helped by the poets, I like to polish up my household words. I administer the joys of the two genders equitably. I imagine that words have little moments of happiness when they are connected from one gender to another—little rivalries too in times of literary malice. Does *l'huis* (m.) or la *porte* (f.) close up the dwelling better? What a lot of "psychological" nuances between the forbidding *huis* and the welcoming *porte*. How could words which are not of the same gender be synonymous? You do not have to like to write in order to see that.

Like the fabulist who recounted the dialogue between the city rat and the field rat, I would like to give voice to the friendly

[30] Proudhon, *loc. cit.*, p. 265.
[31] A monthly newspaper published in Lausanne, December, 1958.

lamp (*lampe,* f.) and the stupid candleabrum (*lampadaire,* m.), that Trissotin[32] of parlor lights. Things see, they talk among themselves, or so thought the good Estaunié who made them tell, like gossipy old women, the drama of the house's occupants. How much more lively and intimate the discussions between the things and objects would be if "each (*chacun,* m.) could find its each (*chacune,* f.)." For words love each other. Like everything that lives, they were "created man and woman."

And thus it is that, in endless reveries, I arouse the matrimonial qualities of my vocabulary. Sometimes in plebeian reveries, I unite the casket (*coffret,* m.) with the earthenware vessel (*terrine,* f.). But the very close synonymies which proceed from the masculine to the feminine delight me. I can't keep from dreaming of them. All my reveries become dualized. Every word, whether it touches on things, the world, sentiments or monsters, goes off looking for its companion: *la glace* (mirror) and *le miroir,* the faithful *montre* (f., watch) and the exact *chronomètre* (m.), *la feuille* (leaf) of the tree and *le feuillet* (leaf of the book), *le bois* (woods) and *la forêt* (forest), *la nuée* (cloud) and *le nuage* (cloud), *la vouivre* (serpent) and *le dragon, le luth* (lute) and *la lyre, les pleurs* (m., tears), and *les larmes* (f., tears). . . .

Sometimes, when I am tired of so many oscillations, I look for refuge in a word which I begin to love for itself. Resting in the heart of words, seeing clearly into the cell of a word, feeling that the word is the seed of a life, a growing dawn . . . The poet says all that in a line: "A word can be a dawn and even a sure shelter." [33]

From then on, what joy in reading, what happiness for the ear when, in reading Mistral, one hears the poet from Provence put the word "cradle" (*berceau,* m.) in the feminine. Wanting to gather some *fleurs de glais* the four-year-old Mistral fell into the pond. His mother pulled him out and put dry clothes on him. But the flowers on the pond are so beautiful that the child makes another slip trying to pick them. For lack of any other clothes, it was necessary to put his Sunday dress on him. In his Sunday dress,

---

[32] A ridiculous character in Molière's comedy *Les femmes savantes* (Translator's note).
[33] Edmond Vandercammen, *La porte sans mémoire,* p. 33.

the temptation is stronger than any admonition, and the child returns to the pond and once more falls into the water. The good mother dries him off with her apron, and, says Mistral, "fearing a fright, she made me drink a spoonful of vermifuge and put me to bed in my *berce* (f.) where, after a little while, I grew tired of crying and fell asleep." [34]

It is essential to read the entire story in the original text. In summarizing, I can only retain the tenderness which is condensed into a word which consoles and helps to sleep. In my cradle, says Mistral, in a *berce,* what great sleep there is for a childhood.

In a *berce,* one knows the true sleep, since one sleeps in the feminine.

VII

One of the greatest sentence workers one day made the following remark: "You have certainly observed the curious fact that a given *word* which is perfectly clear when you hear it or use it in *everyday* language, and which does not give rise to any difficulty when it is engaged in the rapid movement of an ordinary sentence becomes magically embarassing, introduces a strange resistance, frustrates any effort at definition as soon as you take it out of circulation to examine it separately and look for its meaning after taking away its instantaneous function." [35] The words which Valéry takes as examples are two words which, for a long time, have both "played at being important": they are "time" and "life." Taken out of circulation, both of these words immediately take on the aspect of enigmas. But for less ostentatious words, Valéry can very well say "that we understand ourselves thanks only to *the speed of our passages past words*"; [36] reverie, slow reverie discovers the depths in the immobility of a word. We believe that, through reverie, we can discover within a word the act which names.

"Words dream that they are being named," writes a poet.[37]

34 Frederic Mistral, *Mémoires et récits* (translated from the Provençal), Plon, p. 19. [*Berce* is the Provençal word for *berceau* (m.), cradle (Translator's note).]
35 Paul Valéry, *Variété V*, Gallimard, p. 132.
36 *Loc. cit.*, p. 133.
37 Leo Libbrecht, *Mon orgue de Barbarie*, p. 34.

They want someone to dream while naming them. And that quite simply, without digging the abyss of etymologies. In their present being, words, by gathering dreams (*songes*), become realities. What word dreamer could keep from dreaming when he reads these two lines by Louis Emié:

> A word moves about in the shadows
> and swells the draperies.[88]

With these two lines, I would like to conduct a test of oneiric sensitivity as regards the sensitivity to language. It would be necessary to ask: "Don't you believe that certain words have such a sonority that they come to take up space and volume among the beings in the room?" What was really swelling the curtains in Edgar Allen Poe's room, a being, a memory or a noun?

A psychologist with a "clear and distinct" mind would be astonished by Emié's lines. He would at least want someone to tell him what this word was giving animation to the draperies; with a given word, he would perhaps follow through a possible phantomalization. In asking for precise details, the psychologist is not feeling that the poet has just opened up the universe of words to him. The poet's room is full of words, words which move about in the shadows. Sometimes the words are unfaithful to the things. They try to establish oneiric synonymies between things. The phantomalization of objects is always expressed in the language of visual hallucinations. But for a word dreamer there are phantomalizations through language. In order to go to those oneiric depths words must be given the time to dream. And so it is that, while meditating on Valéry's remark, one is led to liberate himself from the teleology of the sentence. Thus, for a word dreamer there are words which are *shells of speech* (*coquilles de parole*). Yes, by listening to certain words as a child listens to the sea in a seashell, a word dreamer hears the murmur of a world of dreams (*songes*).

Still other dreams (*rêves*) are born when, instead of reading or speaking, one writes as he wrote long ago in the days when he was a schoolboy. Taking care to write beautifully, one seems to move toward the interior of words. A letter astonishes; you hadn't heard

---

[88] Louis Emié, *Le nom du feu*, Gallimard, p. 35.

it well while reading. Under the attentive pen, one listens differently. So a poet can write: "Would I know how to set up housekeeping in the curls of consonants which never resound, in the knots of vowels which are never vocalized?" [39]

The following affirmation by a poet bears witness to just how far a letter dreamer can go: "Words are bodies whose members are letters. Their sex is always a vowel." [40]

In the penetrating preface which Gabriel Bounoure wrote for Edmond Jabès' collection of poems, one can read that the poet "knows that a violent, rebellious, sexual, analogical life is deployed in writing and articulation. The changing nuances, the fine and shaded colorations of the feminine vowels are married to the consonants which outline the masculine structure of the vocable. Like us, words have sexes and like us are members of the Logos. Like us they search for their fulfillment in a kingdom of truth; their rebellions, their nostalgias, their affinities, their tendencies, like ours, are magnetized by the archetype of the Androgyne." [41]

In order to dream so far, is it enough to read? Isn't it necessary to write? Write as in our schoolboy past, in those days when, as Bounoure says, the letters wrote themselves one by one, either in their gibbosity or else in their pretentious elegance? In those days, spelling was a drama, our drama of culture at work in the interior of a word. And thus Edmond Jabès gives me back forgotten memories. He writes: "My God, may I know how to spell 'Chrysanthemum' in school tomorrow; from among the different ways of writing this word, may I happen upon the right one. My God, make the letters which deliver it come to my aid; may my schoolmaster understand that it is really a question of the flower he is fond of and not the pyxidium whose carcass I can color at will, the shadow and depth of whose eyes I can cut out and which haunts my reveries." [42]

And this word "chrysanthemum" with so warm an interior,

39 Robert Mallet, *Les signes de l'addition,* p. 156.
40 Edmond Jabès, *Les mots tracent,* edit. Les Pas Perdus, p. 37.
41 Edmond Jabès, *Je bâtis ma demeure,* Preface by Gabriel Bounoure, Gallimard, p. 20.
42 Edmond Jabès, *Je bâtis ma demeure,* p. 336.

what might its gender be? For me this gender depends upon yesterday's Novembers. In my old country, they used to say either *un* or *une*. Without the help of color how could you fix the gender in your ear?

In writing, you discover interior sonorities in words. Diphthongs sound differently beneath the pen. One hears them with their sounds divorced. Is this suffering? Is it a new voluptuousness? Who will tell us the painful delights which the poet finds by slipping a hiatus into the very heart of a word? Listen to the sufferings of a line by Mallarmé where each hemistich has its conflict between vowels: "Pour ouir dans la chair pleurer le diamant" (To hear in its flesh the diamond crying). The diamond breaks into three pieces revealing the fragility of its name. And in this way the sadism of a great poet comes to the surface.

By reading too rapidly, the line becomes decasyllabic. But when my pen spells, the line regains its twelve syllables, and the ear is obliged to the noble work of a rare alexandrine.

But such great words of musicality in verse surpass the knowledge (*savoir*) of a dreamer. Our word reveries do not descend to the depths of the vocables, and we only know how to speak lines in an interior speech. Decidedly, we are nothing more than an adept of solitary reading.[48]

VIII

Having admitted—doubtless with too much complacency—these vagabond thoughts which turn about an obsession, these madnesses (*vésanies*) which multiply in times of reverie, may I be permitted to indicate their place in my life as an intellectual workman.

If I were to summarize an irregular and laborious career marked by various books, the best thing would be to situate it under the contradictory signs, masculine and feminine, of the *concept* (m.) and the *image* (f.). Between the concept and the image, there is no synthesis. And there is no filiation either; and above all not that filiation which is always talked about and never experienced by which psychologists make the concept pro-

---

[48] Some time ago we wrote a chapter entitled: "Mute Declamation." Cf. *L'air et les songes*, Paris, Corti.

ceed from a plurality of images. Whoever gives himself over to the concept with all his mind, over to the image with all his soul, knows perfectly well that concepts and images develop on two divergent planes of the spiritual life.

Perhaps it is even a good idea to stir up a rivalry between conceptual and imaginative activity. In any case, one will encounter nothing but disappointments if he intends to make them cooperate. The image can not provide matter for a concept. By giving stability to the image, the concept would stifle its life.

And it is not I who shall try to weaken the clear polarity between the intellect and the imagination by confusional transactions. Once I felt duty-bound to write a book to exorcise the images which claim to engender and maintain concepts in a· scientific culture.[44] When the concept has taken up its essential activity, that is to say when it functions in a concept field, what softness—what femininity!—there would be to use images. In the strong tissue of rational thought there intervene inter-concepts, or concepts which only take on their sense and their rigor in their rational relationships. We have given examples of these inter-concepts in our book, *The Applied Rationalism*. In scientific thought, the concept functions all the better for being cut off from all background images (*arrière-image*). In its full exercise, the scientific concept is free from all the delays of its genetic evolution, an evolution which is consequently explained by simple psychology.

The virility of knowledge (*savoir*) increases with each conquest of the constructive abstraction, whose action is so different from that described in psychology books. The organizational force of abstract thought in mathematics is manifest. As Nietzsche says: "In mathematics. . . , absolute knowledge (*connaissance*) celebrates its Saturnalia." [45]

Whoever gives himself over with enthusiasm to rational thought can turn away from the smoke (*fumées*, f.) and mists

---

[44] Cf. *La formation de l'esprit scientifique. Contribution à une psychanalyse de la connaissance scientifique*, 3rd edition, Vrin (Paris, 1954).
[45] Nietzsche, *La naissance de la philosophie à l'époque de la tragédie grecque*, translated by G. Bianquis, Gallimard, p. 204.

(*brumes,* f.) by means of which irrationalists try to surround with doubt the active light of well-associated concepts.

Smoke and mists, an objection of the feminine.

But, on the other hand, neither will it be I who, telling my faithful love for images, will study them with great support from concepts. Intellectualist criticism of poetry will never lead to the source (*foyer*) where poetic images take form. One must keep from giving commands to the image as a mesmerizer gives commands to the somnambulist.[46] In order to know the success of images, it is better to follow the somnambulistic reverie, to listen, as Nodier did, to the dreamer's somniloquy. The image can only be studied through the image, by dreaming images as they gather in reverie. It is a non-sense to claim to study imagination objectively since one really receives the image only if he admires it. Already in comparing one image to another, one runs the risk of losing participation in its individuality.

Thus, images and concepts take form at those two opposite poles of psychic activity which are imagination and reason. Between them there is a polarity of exclusion at work. They have nothing in common with the poles of magnetism. Here, the opposing poles do not attract; they repel. One must love the psychic forces of two different types of love if he loves concepts and images, the masculine and feminine poles of the Psyche. I understood that too late. Too late, I came to know the clear conscience in work alternating between images and concepts, two clear consciences which would be that of broad daylight and that which accepts the nocturnal side of the soul. For me to enjoy a double clear conscience, the clear conscience of my double nature finally recognized, I would have to write two more books: a book on applied rationalism and a book on active imagination. As insufficient as works may be, a clear conscience is, for me, an occu-

---

46 Ritter wrote to Franz von Baader: "Everyone carries within him his somnambulist of whom he is the mesmerizer." (Quoted by Beguin, *L'âme romantique et le rêve,* Cahiers du Sud, vol. I, p. 144.) When the reverie is good, when it has the continuum of good things, it is the somnambulist in us who imperceptibly commands the action of his mesmerizer.

pied conscience[47]—never empty—the conscience of a man at work until his last breath.

---

[47] Or "consciousness." There seems to be a sustained conceit or play on meanings at work in this last paragraph around the word *conscience* meaning "conscience" and "consciousness," often at the same time (Translator's note).

ক্ষ ক্ষ *Two*

Reveries on Reverie
(*"Animus"* - *"Anima"*)

Why are you never alone with me
Deep woman, deeper than the abyss
To which the sources of the past are attached?

The more I approach you, the more you sink
Into the ravine of preexistences.

> Yvan Goll,
> *Multiple femme*

I have the soul of a faun and an
adolescent girl, very much at once.

> Francis Jammes,
> *Le roman du lièvre*

I

In telling our daydreamings (*songeries,* f.) on the masculine and feminine of words as simply as we have just done, with the innocence of a philosopher, we are well aware that we are only suggesting a surface psychology. Such remarks playing on vocabulary cannot attract the attention of psychologists who make an effort to tell, in a precise and stable language, what they observe objectively in the very ideal of the scientific spirit. For them, words do not dream. Even if the psychologist were sensitive to our indications, he would not fail to tell us that the poor verbal designations of genders run the risk of appearing to be an inflation of the values of the masculine and the feminine. By using some ready-made formula, people will find it easy to object that we are abandoning the thing for the sign and that the characteristics of femininity and virility are so deeply inscribed in human nature that night dreams themselves know the dramas of opposing sexualities. But here, as in many other passages of this essay, we shall oppose the dream (*rêve,* m.) and the reverie (*rêverie,* f.). Then in our love affairs in speech (*amours en parole*), in the reveries where we prepare the words (*paroles*) we shall speak to the absent woman, the words (*mots*), the beautiful words take on a full life, and some day it will be quite necessary for a psychologist to get around to studying life in speech (*la vie en parole*), life which takes on meaning in speaking.

We believe we can also show that words do not have exactly the

same psychic "weight" depending on whether they belong to the
language of reverie or to the language of daylight life (*la vie
claire*)—to rested language or language under surveillance—to
the language of natural poetry or to the language hammered out
by authoritarian prosodies. The nocturnal dream can well be a
violent or crafty battle against censures. Reverie can help us know
language without censorship. In solitary reverie we can tell ourselves everything. Our consciousness is still clear enough that we
are sure that what we are saying to ourselves is really being said
only to ourselves.

It is in no way astonishing then that in solitary reverie we know
ourselves in the feminine and the masculine at the same time.
Reverie which lives out the future of a passion idealizes the object
of its passion. The ideal feminine being listens to the passionate
dreamer (*rêveur*, m.). The dreaming woman elicits the declara-
tions of an idealized man. In the following chapters we shall come
back to this idealizing character of certain reveries. This idealizing psychology is an undeniable psychic reality. The reverie
idealizes both its object and the dreamer at the same time. And
when the reverie lives in a dualism of the masculine and the feminine, the idealization is concrete and limitless at the same time.

In order to know ourselves doubly as a real being and an idealizing being, we must *listen to* our reveries. We believe that our
reveries can be the best school for the "psychology of the depths."
All the lessons we have learned from the psychology of the depths
will be applied in order to understand the existentialism of reverie better.

A complete psychology which does not favor any one element
of the human psychism must take into account the most extreme
idealization, the one which reaches the region we have described
in an earlier book as the *absolute sublimation*. In other words, a
complete psychology must reintegrate with the human that which
detaches itself from the human—unite the poetics of reverie with
the prosaism of life.

II

In fact, it seems to us unquestionable that an utterance (*parole*, f.) remains attached to the most distant, to the most obscure

desires which stir the human psychism in its depths. The subconscious is ceaselessly murmuring, and it is by listening to these murmurs that one hears its truth. Sometimes desires carry on a dialogue within us—desires? memories perhaps or reminiscences made out of unfinished dreams?—a man and a woman are speaking in the solitude of our being. And in free reverie, they speak in order to admit their desires, to communicate in the tranquility of a well harmonized double nature. Never to do battle. If this intimate man and woman preserve a trace of rivalry, it is because we are dreaming badly, because we are putting everyday names on the creatures of reverie which are outside of time. The farther one descends into the depths of the *speaking being*, the more simply the essential otherness of any speaking being designates itself as the otherness of the masculine and the feminine.

Of all the schools of contemporary psychoanalysis, that of C. G. Jung has shown most clearly that the human psychism is, in its primitive state, androgynous. For Jung, the subconscious self is not a repressed consciousness, it is not made of forgotten memories; it is a primary nature. The subconscious, then, maintains within us forces of androgyneity. Whoever speaks of androgyneity is brushing the depths of his own subconsciousness with a double antenna. One thinks he is telling a story, but the story is interesting to such an extent that it becomes psychology happening. So why did Nietzsche report that "Empedocles remembered being . . . boy and girl?" [1] Does this astonish Nietzsche? Doesn't he see in this Empedoclean memory a token of the depth of meditation of one of the heroes of thought? Is this a useful text for "understanding" Empedocles? Does this text help us descend into the unfathomable depths of the human? And another question: with regard to a text quoted objectively, as by a historian, was Nietzsche involved in a parallel reverie? Is it by reliving the times when the philosopher was "boy-girl" that we shall discover a line of inquiry for "analyzing" the virility of the super-human? Ah! really what are philosophers dreaming of?

Faced with such great dreams (*songes*), can one be simply a psychologist? Not everything will have been said when it is re-

---

[1] Nietzsche, *loc. cit.*, p. 142.

called that Nietzsche never forgot what was, for him, that strange, lost paradise of a Protestant presbytery filled with feminine presences. Nietzsche's femininity is deeper for being more hidden. Who is there under the super-masculine mask of Zarathustra? With regard to women, there are, in Nietzsche's work, little disdains in bad taste. Beneath all these coverings and compensations, who will discover the feminine Nietzsche for us? And who will found the Nietzscheism of the feminine?

Since we are limiting our inquiries to the world of reverie, we can certainly say that in man as in woman, harmonious androgyneity keeps its role of maintaining the calming action of reverie. Conscious and consequently vigorous demands manifestly trouble this psychic repose. They are, then, manifestations of a rivalry between the masculine and the feminine at the moment they are both detaching themselves from the primitive androgyneity. From the moment it leaves its haunts—like that of profound reverie—the androgyneity becomes unbalanced. It then falls prey to oscillations. Psychology takes note of these oscillations as a sign of abnormality. But when the reverie deepens, these oscillations die down, and the psychism finds *the peace of genders* again, that peace which the word dreamer knows.

In his fine book, *The Woman*,[2] the psychologist Buytendijk gives a reference where he says that the normal man is 51 per cent masculine and that the woman is 51 per cent feminine. Obviously, these figures are given for the sake of polemic, to ruin the tranquil assurance of the two parallel monoliths of the integral masculine and the integral feminine. But time works on all the proportions; day, night, seasons, and ages do not leave our balanced androgyneity in peace. In each human being, the clock of masculine hours and the clock of feminine hours do not belong to the realm of figures and measurements. The clock of the feminine runs continuously in a duration which peacefully slips away. The masculine clock has the dynamism of jerks. One would feel this better if he agreed to set up reverie and the efforts of knowledge in a frank dialectic.

Furthermore, that is not a really parallel dialectic, operating at

---

2 F. J. J. Buytendijk, *loc. cit.*, p. 79.

one single level like the poor dialectic between yea's and nay's. The dialectic of the masculine and the feminine unfolds on an in-depth rhythm. It goes from the less deep, ever less deep (the masculine) to the ever deep, ever deeper (the feminine). It is in reverie, "in the inexhaustible reserve of latent life," as Henri Bosco says,[3] that we find the feminine deployed in all its breadth, reposing in its simple tranquility. Then, as it must be reborn with the coming of the day, the clock of the intimate being rings in the masculine—in the masculine for everyone, men and women. Then, for everyone, the times of social activity return, an activity which is essentially masculine. And even in love life, men and women both know how to use their double force. That poses a new, difficult problem, that of establishing or maintaining the harmony of their double gender in each of the two partners.

When genius intervenes in the determinations of the forces of *animus* and *anima* in one and the same soul, a dominant sign imposes a personal unity on the duality. When Milosz, "who prides himself on writing with the soul of words," writes the word "love," he knows that this word contains "the eternal divine-feminine of Alighieri and Goethe, the angelic sentimentality and sensuality, the virginal maternity where, as in a burning crucible, Swedenborg's adramandonic, Hölderlin's hesperic and Schiller's elyssian are melted together: the perfect human harmony, formed by the attracting wisdom of the husband and the loving gravitation of the wife, the real spiritual situation of the one in the eye of the other, essential arcanum, so terrible and beautiful that, from the day I penetrated it, it became impossible for me to speak of it without shedding a torrent of tears." This text, taken from the *Epistle to Storge* is quoted in the fine study of Milosz by Jean Cassou.[4] Milosz does not gather geniuses together here without a good reason. From one poet to another, the syntheses of *animus* and *anima* are different, but these syntheses are in opposition precisely because they are all under the sign of the essential synthesis, the more far-reaching synthesis which unites the forces of *animus* and *anima* in a single arcanum. Such syntheses with so wide a scope, such syntheses sealed so high within the superhu-

---

[3] Henri Bosco, *Un rameau de la nuit.* Paris, Flammarion, p. 13.
[4] Jean Cassou, *Trois poètes: Rilke, Milosz, Machado,* edit. Plon, p. 77.

man, are easily destroyed upon contact with daily life. But one feels them taking form, or changing form perhaps, when he listens to the great dreamers of human greatness cited by Milosz.

III

So that there would be no confusion with the realities of surface psychology, C. G. Jung had the excellent idea of situating the masculine and the feminine of the depths under the double sign of two Latin substantives, *anima* and *animus*. Two substantives for one single soul are necessary in order to communicate the reality of the human psychism. The most virile man, too simply characterized by a strong *animus,* also has an *anima*—an *anima* which can have paradoxical manifestations. In the same way, the most feminine women also has psychic determinations which prove the existence of an *animus* within her.[5] Modern social life with its competitions which "mix the genders" teaches us to curb the manifestations of androgyny. But in our reveries, in the great solitude of our reveries, when we are so profoundly liberated that we no longer even think of the virtual rivalries, our entire soul is impregnated with the influence of the *anima*.

And here we are at the very core of the thesis we wish to defend in the present essay: *reverie is under the sign of the anima*. When the reverie is truly profound, the being who comes to dream within us is our *anima*.

For a philosopher who takes his inspiration from phenomenology, a reverie on reverie is very exactly a phenomenology of the *anima,* and it is by coordinating reveries on reverie that he hopes to constitute a "Poetics of reverie." In other words, the poetics of reverie is a poetics of the *anima*.

In order to avoid any false interpretation, let us recall that our essay does not claim to include a poetics of the nocturnal dream (*rêve,* m.) any more than a poetics of the fantastic. This poetics of the fantastic would require great attention to the intellectuality

---

5 This double determination has not always been maintained in all its symmetry in the course of Jung's numerous books. Yet the reference to such a symmetry is very useful in a psychological examination. Sometimes it helps uncover barely visible psychological traces which are, however, active in free reveries.

of the fantastic. We are limiting ourselves to a study of reverie.

On the other hand, by agreeing to the reference to two psycho-logical instances, *anima* and *animus,* in order to classify our re-flections on the essential femininity of any deep reverie, we are, we believe, protecting ourselves from an objection. One could, in fact, object—by following the automatism from which so many philosophical dialectics suffer—that if the man centered on the *animus* dreams the reverie in *anima,* the woman centered on the *anima* should dream in *animus.* Doubtless, the tension of civiliza-tion is presently such that "feminism" commonly reinforces the *animus* of the woman . . . It has been repeated often enough that feminism ruins femininity. But once again, if one wishes to give reverie its fundamental character, if he wishes to take it as a state, a present state which has no need for the scaffolding of *projects,* it is necessary to recognize that reverie liberates any dreamer, man or woman, from the world of demands. Reverie goes in the opposite direction from any demand. In a pure reverie which returns the dreamer to his tranquil solitude, every human being, man or woman, finds his repose in the *anima* of the depths, by descending, ever descending "the slope of reverie." A descent without fall. In those indeterminate depths reigns the repose of the feminine. It is in this feminine repose, away from worries, ambitions, and projects that we know concrete repose, the repose which reposes our whole being. Whoever knows this concrete re-pose where soul and body bathe in the tranquility of reverie understands the truth of the paradox put forth by George Sand who said: "The days are made to repose us from our nights; that is to say, the reveries of the lucid day are made to rest us from our dreams of the night." [6] For the repose of sleep refreshes only the body. It rarely sets the soul at rest. The repose of the night does not belong to us. It is not the possession of our being. Sleep opens within us an inn for phantoms. In the morning we must sweep out the shadows; through psychoanalysis, lingering visitors must be dislodged, and we must even scare out, from the bottom of

[6] Ernest La Jeunesse said (*L'imitation de notre maître Napoléon,* p. 45): "Sleeping is the most tiring function there is." Reverie assimilates the night-mares of the night. It is the natural psychoanalyst of our nocturnal dramas, of our subconscious dramas.

abysses, monsters from another age, the dragon and the serpent, all those animal coagulations of the masculine and the feminine, unassimilated and unassimilable.

Quite to the contrary, daytime reverie benefits from a lucid tranquility. Even if it is tinged with melancholy, that melancholy is restful, it is an engaging melancholy which gives a continuity to our repose.

One might be tempted to think that this lucid tranquility is simply the awareness of an absence of worries. But the reverie would not last if it were not nourished by the images of the sweetness of living, by the illusions of happiness. A dreamer's reverie is sufficient to make an entire universe dream. The dreamer's repose is sufficient to put the waters, clouds and the gentle breeze to rest. At the threshhold of a great book, where he was to dream a great deal, Henri Bosco writes: "I was happy. Nothing detached itself from my pleasure but limpid water, the trembling of leaves, the fragrant cloth of young smoke, breezes from the hills." [7] So reverie is not a mind vacuum. It *is* rather the gift of an hour which knows the plenitude of the soul.

Thus, projects and worries, two ways of not being present to oneself, belong to the *animus*. Reverie which lives the present of happy images belongs to the *anima*. In happy hours we know a reverie which feeds on itself, which maintains itself in the same way life maintains itself. The tranquil images, gifts from this great insouciance which is the essence of the feminine, sustain and balance themselves in the peace of the *anima*. These images melt together in an intimate warmth, in the constant softness where the nucleus of the feminine bathes in every soul. Since it is the thesis which is guiding our research, let us repeat that pure reverie, filled with images, is a manifestation of the *anima*, perhaps the most characteristic manifestation. In any case, it is in the realm of images that we, the dreaming (*songeur*) philosopher, look for the *anima* benefits. Water images give any dreamer ecstasies (*ivresses*) of femininity. Whoever is marked by water remains faithful to his *anima*. And in general, the great simple images

---

[7] Henri Bosco, *Un rameau de la nuit*, p. 13.

captured at their birth in a sincere reverie very often tell of their *anima* quality.

But where could we, the solitary philosopher, gather these images? In life or in books? In our personal life, such images would only be our own poor images. And unlike psychologists of observation, we are not in contact with a great enough number of "natural" documents to determine the reverie of the man in the street. So here we are confined to our role as a psychologist of reading. But happily for our investigations into books, if we really receive images in *anima*, the poets' images, they appear to us as documents of natural reverie. Almost as soon as we receive them, we are imagining that we could have dreamed them. Poetic images stimulate our reverie; they melt into our reverie because the power of assimilation of the *anima* is so great. We were reading and now we are dreaming. An image received in the *anima* puts us in a state of continuous reverie. Throughout our work we shall be giving many examples of reading reveries, so many evasions which do not conform to the duty of an objective literary critic.

In sum, it must be admitted that there are two types of reading: reading in *animus* and reading in *anima*. I am not the same man when I am reading a book of ideas where the *animus* is obliged to be vigilant, quite ready to criticize, quite ready to retort, as when I am reading a poet's book where images must be received in a sort of transcendental acceptance of gifts. Ah! to return the absolute gift which is a poet's image, our *anima* would have to be able to write a hymn of thanksgiving.[8]

The *animus* reads little; the *anima* reads a great deal.

Sometimes my *animus* scolds me for having read too much.

Reading, ever reading, the sweet passion of the *anima*. But

---

[8] A propos of a story by Goethe on the hunt which "the severe Gervinus" considered "unspeakably insignificant," the translator of Eckermann's book, Emile Délérot, points out (*Conversations de Goethe*, translation vol. I, p. 268 note): "Yet Goethe affirms to us that he carried it around in himself *thirty years*. To find it worthy of its author, it must be read in the German manner, that is to say, in giving it a long commentary of reveries. Works which please the German taste most are those which can best serve as a starting point for endless dreams (*songes*)."

when, after having read everything, one sets before himself the task of making a book out of reveries, it is the *animus* which is in the harness. Writing a book is always a hard job. One is always tempted to limit himself to dreaming it.

IV

The *anima,* back to which the reveries of repose lead us, is not always well defined by its outcroppings in everyday life. The symptoms of femininity which the psychologist enumerates in order to determine his characterological classifications do not put us in veritable contact with the *normal anima,* the *anima* which resides in every *normal* human being. Often the psychologist notices only the froth of the fermentations of a troubled *anima,* tormented by "problems." Problems! As if there were problems for the man who knows the security of feminine repose!

In the psychiatrists' clinics, in spite of all the anomalies, the man-woman dialectic remains bulwarked by traits in too sharp contrast. Under the two signs of the physiological sexual division, man seems to divide himself too brutally for anyone to initiate a psychology of tenderness, of the double tenderness, the tenderness of *animus* and the tenderness of *anima.* And that is why, in a desire not to fall victim to simplistic physiological designations, the psychologists of the depths have been led to speak of the *anima-animus* dialectic, a dialectic which permits greater nuance in psychological studies than the strict male-female opposition.

But everything is not said when one creates words. With new words, it is necessary to keep from speaking the old language. It would be well here not to remain within a parallelistic designation. A geometer would suggest defining the relationship between *animus* and *anima* as two antiparallel developments which would be the same as saying that the *animus* becomes clear and reigns in a psychic growth while the *anima* becomes deeper and reigns in descending toward the cave of the being. By descending, ever descending, the ontology of the qualities of the *anima* is discovered. In everyday life, the words "man" and "woman"—dresses and pants—are sufficient designations. But in the muted life of the subconscious, in the retiring life of a solitary dreamer, peremptory designations lose their authority. The words *animus* and *anima* have been chosen to soften the sexual designations and escape the simplicity of birth certificate classifications. Yes, it is necessary to keep from putting habitual thoughts back too quickly under the words which come to the aid of our dreams (*songes*). The greatest writers let themselves be taken in. When Claudel announces "a parable of *Animus* and *Anima,* in order to help understand certain poems by Arthur Rimbaud," he evokes no more, in the end, with these terms than the duality of the mind and the soul. And then too, the mind-*animus* is very close to being a body, a wretched body which is going to weigh down all spirituality. "Basically," says the poet, "*Animus* is a bourgeois with regular habits; he likes the same dishes. But . . . one day as *Animus* was coming home unexpectedly, or perhaps was dozing after dinner, or perhaps was absorbed in his work, he heard *Anima* who was singing all alone behind the closed door: a curious song, something he did not know." [9] And the Claudelian "parable" pulls up short to permit a discussion of alexandrines.

From it all, let us just retain one ray of light: it is *Anima* who dreams and sings. Dreaming and singing, that is the work of its solitude. Reverie—not the dream (*rêve*)—is the free expansion of all *anima*. It is doubtless with the reveries of his *anima* that the poet manages to give his *animus* ideas the structure of a song, the force of a song.

From that point on, how can we read what the poet has written in an *anima* reverie without *anima* reverie? And that is how I justify not being able to read poets except by dreaming.

V

Thus, always with the reveries of others, read with the slowness of our reader's reveries—never in ordinary psychology—we must outline an *anima* philosophy, a philosophy of the psychology of the deep feminine. Pehaps our limited means provide us with a guarantee of remaining a philosopher. Fundamentally, considered in ordinary life, the *anima* would hardly be anything more than the worthy bourgeois wife linked to this bourgeois *animus* which Paul Claudel presents us with. Often a psychology which is

---

[9] Paul Claudel, *Positions et propositions,* vol. I, p. 56.

too obvious offends the philosopher's gaze. The psychology of men poses an obstacle to the philosophy of men. Thus, C. G. Jung who has shed so much light on the *anima* in the course of his studies of the cosmic reveries of men like Paracelsus, of the criss-crossed cosmicities of the *animus* and the *anima* in alchemical meditations, Jung himself seems to us to accept a detonalization of his philosophical thoughts when he is studying the *anima* in his clientele. We have all known men who are authoritarian in their social functions—some military man with his rigid kepi—but who become very humble in the evening upon returning to the authority of the wife or aged mother. With these "contradic-tions" in character, novelists create facile novels, novels which we all understand, which clearly proves that the novelist is speaking the truth, that the "psychological observation" is correct. But if psychology is written for everyone, philosophy can only be writ-ten for the few. Those swellings of being which man receives from great social functions are only rough psychological determina-tions; they do not necessarily correspond to an outline of the being which would interest the philosopher. The psychologist is right in taking an interest in them. He must take them into ac-count in his study of the "environment" (*milieu*). They will be grateful to him, that corporation of the new users of psychology who sort out the elements coming from the human whole in order to classify them in the various levels of a trade. But from the point of view of the philosophy of the in-depth man, man in soli-tude, isn't it necessary to be on guard that such simple, obvious determinations do not impede the study of a subtle ontology? Do accidents reveal substance? Even if Jung tells us that Bismarck had crying spells,[10] such failings of the *animus* do not automatically provide us with positive manifestations of the *anima*. The *anima* *is not a weakness.* One does not find it in a syncope of the *animus*. It has its own forces. It is the interior principle of our repose. Why would this repose come at the end of an avenue of regrets, of sadness, at the end of an avenue of weariness? Why would the tears of the *animus,* Bismarck's tears be the sign of a repressed *anima?*

---

[10] C. G. Jung, *Le Moi et l'inconscient,* translated by Adamov. One chapter is entitled "The *Anima* and the *Animus.*"

Besides there are worse signs than the tears one sheds: there are *written tears*. In the good old days of the "ink spots" during his easy youth, Barrès wrote to Rachilde: "Amidst solitude and my sobbings, I have sometimes discovered more real voluptuousness than in the arms of a woman." [11] Is that a document which can sensitize the boundaries between the *animus* and the *anima* in the author of *The Garden of Bérénice?* Must this document be believed when it is so difficult to imagine?

Isn't it striking that more often than not the contradictions between the *animus* and the *anima* give rise to ironic judgments? Irony gives us, at little expense, the impression that we are experienced psychologists. On the other hand, we end up believing only those cases worthy of our attention where, through our irony, we are first of all assured of our "objectivity." But psychological observation distinguishes, divides. In order to participate in the unions of the *animus* and *anima*, it would be necessary to know *dreaming observation*, and every born observer holds that to be a monstrosity.

In order to receive the positive forces of the *anima*, we believe, then, that it would be necessary to turn our backs on the inquiries of psychologists who go chasing after injured psychisms. The *anima* feels repugnance toward accidents. It is soft substance, harmonious (*unie*) substance which wishes to enjoy its harmonious being slowly, softly. We shall live more surely in *anima* by deepening reverie, by loving reverie, above all the reverie of water, in the great repose of still waters. O beautiful water without sin which renews the *anima* purities in the idealizing reverie! Before the world thus simplified by a water in its repose, the consciousness of a dreaming soul is simple. The phenomenology of simple and pure reverie opens a path to us which leads us to a psychism without blemish, toward the psychism of our repose. Reverie before still waters gives us that experience of a permanent psychic consistency which is the possession of the *anima*. Here we receive the teachings of a *natural calm* and an entreaty to become conscious of the calm of our own nature, of the substantial calm of our *anima*. The *anima*, the principle of our re-

---

11 Fragment of a letter from Barrès to Rachilde quoted by Rachilde herself in the chapter she devoted to Barrès in her book, *Portraits d'hommes*, 1929, p. 24.

pose, is that nature within us which is sufficient unto itself;[12] it is the tranquil feminine. The *anima,* the principle of our profound reveries, is really the being of our still water within us.

VI

If we are reticent to use the *animus-anima* dialectic in ordinary psychology, we continuously feel its efficiency when we follow Jung in his studies of the great cosmic reveries of alchemy. Through alchemy, a whole field of reveries which think and of thoughts which dream is opened to the psychologist who is willing to grasp the principles of a *studious animism.* The alchemist's animism does not settle for expressing itself in general hymns about life. The animistic convictions of the alchemist are not centered on an immediate participation as in natural, simple animism. Here studious animism is an animism which experiments with itself, which multiplies itself in innumerable experiments. In his laboratory, the alchemist puts his reveries into experiments.

From then on, the language of alchemy is a language of reverie, the mother tongue of cosmic reverie. This language must be learned as it has been dreamed, in solitude. *One is never so alone as when he is reading a book of alchemy.* One gets the impression that he is "the only person in the world." And immediately he dreams the world; he speaks the language of the beginnings of the world.

In order to recover such dreams (*songes*), to understand such a language, it is quite essential to take care to desocialize the terms of everyday language. A reversal must then be made in order to give full reality to the metaphor. What a lot of exercises that makes for a word dreamer! The metaphor is then an origin, the origin of an image which acts directly, immediately. If the King and the Queen in alchemical reverie come to watch the formation of a substance, they are not coming only to preside at a marriage of the elements. They are not simply emblems for the grandeur of

---

[12] Studying the physics of love in his own way, with more cynicism than poetry, Rémy de Gourmont writes: "The male is an accident; the female would have been enough" (*La physique de l'amour,* Mercure de France, p. 73). Cf. also Buytendijk, *La Femme,* p. 39.

the work. They are truly the majesties of the masculine and the feminine working at a cosmic creation. All of a sudden we are transported to the summit of differentiated *animism*. In their great actions, the living masculine and feminine are king and queen.

Under the sign of the double crown of the king and the queen, while the king and the queen cross their fleur-de-lis, the masculine and feminine forces of the cosmos are uniting. Queen and King are sovereigns without reality if they are isolated. The King and the Queen of the alchemist are the *Animus* and the *Anima* of the World, magnified images of the *animus* and the *anima* of the dreaming (*songeur*) alchemist. And these principles are very close in the world just as they are close within us.

In alchemy, the conjunctions of the masculine and the feminine are complex. One never quite knows at what level the unions are being made. Many texts quoted by Jung tell of so many moments of incestuousness. Who will help us realize all the nuances of alchemical reveries in a work on genders when it is a question of the union of brother and sister, Apollo and Diana, of the Sun and the Moon? What an expansion of laboratory experiments it is when one can put the work under the sign of such great names, when one can put the affinities of substances under the sign of such dear relationships! A positive mind—some historian of alchemy wishing to find, beneath texts of exaltation, some of the rudiments of science—will continually "reduce" the language. But such texts have been living by their language. And the psychologist can not be fooled; the language of the alchemist is a passionate language, a language which can only be understood as the dialogue between an *anima* and an *animus* united in the soul of the dreamer.

An immense word reverie runs through alchemy. Here in their omnipotence are revealed the masculine and the feminine of words given to inanimate objects and primordial substances.

What action could bodies and substances have if they were not named in a further increase of dignity where common nouns become proper nouns? Rare will be the substances with a versatile sexuality: they have a role which an alert sexologist could elucidate. In any case, the *animus* has one vocabulary and the *anima* has another. Anything can be born from the union of two vocabularies when one follows the reveries of the speaking being. Things, substances, and stars must obey the prestige of their name.

These names are words of praise or scorn, but nearly always of praise. In any event, the vocabulary of abuse is shorter. The curse breaks the reverie. In alchemy it is the sign of a failure. When the forces of matter must be awakened, praise is sovereign. Let us remember that praise has a magical action. That is evident in the psychology of men. It ought then to be the same in a psychology of matter which gives substances human forces and desires. In his book *Servius and Fortune,* Dumézil writes (p. 67): "Thus covered with praise, Indra began to grow."

Matter, to which one speaks according to the rules when he is working it, swells under the hand of the workman. This *anima* accepts the flatteries of the *animus* which make it emerge from its torpor. The hands dream. Between the hand and the things, a whole psychology unfolds. In this psychology clear ideas play a minor role. They really remain in the periphery, following, as Bergson says, the dotted line of our habitual actions. For things as for souls, the mystery is inside. A reverie of intimacy—of an intimacy which is always human—opens up for the man who enters into the mysteries of matter.

If in examining alchemical books today, one does not receive all the resonances of spoken reverie, he risks falling victim to a transposed objectivity. In effect, caution must be taken not to give substances conceived as being secretly animate the statutes of the inanimate world of today's science. One must then ceaselessly reconstitute the complex of ideas and reveries. In order to do that, it is proper to read every book of alchemy twice, as a psychologist and as a historian of science. Jung happily chose to entitle his study *Psychologie und Alchemie.* And the psychology of the alchemist is that of reveries trying to constitute themselves in experiments on the exterior world. A double vocabulary must be established between reverie and experiment. The *exaltation* of the names of substances is the preamble to experiments on the "exalted" substances. Alchemical gold is a reification of a strange need for royalty, superiority and domination which animates the *animus* of the solitary alchemist. The dreamer does not want gold for some distant social use, but for an *immediate* psychological use, to be king in the majesty of his *animus*. For the alchemist is a dreamer who wishes, who enjoys wishing, who magnifies himself in his "wishing big." By invoking gold—that gold which is going to be born in the cave of the dreamer—the alchemist demands of gold, as was long ago demanded of Indra, to "take effect" (*faire vigueur*). And thus it is that alchemical reverie brings about a vigorous psychism. Ah! how masculine that "gold" is!

And the words go to the fore, always to the fore, attracting, drawing, encouraging—exclaiming pride and hope at the same time. The spoken reverie of substances calls matter to birth, to life, to spirituality. Here *literature* is directly active (*agissante*). Without it everything dies out, facts lose the halo of their values.

And thus it is that alchemy is a *solemn* science. In all its meditations, the alchemist's *animus* lives in a world of solemnity.

VII

In a psychology of the communion between two persons in love, the dialectic of the *animus* and the *anima* appears as the phenomenon of "psychological projection." The man who loves a woman "projects" upon that woman all the values which he venerates in his own *anima*. And in the same way, the woman "projects" upon the man she loves all the values which her own *animus* would like to conquer.

When they are well-balanced, these two crisscrossed "projections" make for strong unions. When one or the other of these "projections" is disappointed by the reality, then the dramas of a wasted life begin. But these dramas are of little interest to us in the present study we are making of imagined, imaginary life. Very precisely, reverie always opens up for us the possibility of abstracting ourselves from conjugal dramas. One of the functions of reverie is to liberate us from the burdens of life. A veritable instinct for reverie is active within our *anima;* it is this instinct for reverie which gives the psyche continuity in its repose.[13] Here the psychology of idealization is our only task. The poetics of

---

[13] "Love in the weak sex is the instinct of this weakness," quoted by Amédée Pichot, *Les poètes amoureux*, p. 97.

reverie must give body to all the reveries of idealization. It is not enough to characterize, as psychologists ordinarily do, the reveries of idealization as flights from reality. The irreality function takes on its concrete use in a very coherent idealization, in an idealized life which keeps the heart warm, which gives a real dynamism to life. The masculine ideal projected by the *animus* of the woman and the feminine ideal projected by the man's *anima* are pliant forces which can surmount the obstacles of reality. People love each other in complete ideality; each charges his partner with the task of realizing the ideality as he has dreamed it. Thus, in the secret of solitary reveries, it is not shadows which take on animation but the glimmers which light up the dawning of a love.

Thus, in describing the real, a psychologist would be giving a reasonable place to the reality of idealizing forces as soon as he put all the potentialities designated by the *animus-anima* dialectic at the origin of every human psychism; he would have to establish quadripolar relationships between two psychisms which each include a potentiality of *animus* and a potentiality of *anima*. A subtle psychological study, one which forgets nothing, no more reality than idealization, must analyze the psychology of the communion between two souls according to the following diagram:

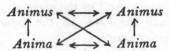

It is upon this keyboard of four beings in two persons that the good and the bad of all close human relationships must be studied. Of course, the multiple bonds between the two *animi* and the two *animae* becomes taut or slack, weaken or are reinforced following the peripeteia of a life. They are living bonds, and the psychologist should be endlessly measuring their tension.

In fact, the reverie of the imagining psychology in every novelist follows the multiple projections which allow him to live in turn in *animus* and in *anima* inside the person of his different characters. The loves of Félix and Mme de Mortsauf in *The Lily in the Valley* reverberate on every string of the quadripolar relationships, above all in the first half of the book where Balzac knew how to maintain a *novel of reveries*. This novel of reveries is so well-balanced that I have difficulty reading the end of the book. In the last part, Félix's *animus* seems artificial to me, an *animus* which comes from somewhere else and which the novelist has imposed upon his character. In the work, Louis XVIII's court appears as a fable of nobility which I have difficulty associating with the profound and simple life of the first Félix. There, we see an excrescence of *animus* which deforms his true character.

But in bringing such judgments to bear, I am adventuring onto ground which does not belong to me. I do not know how to dream on a novel while following the entire story line. In such narratives, I find such an enormity of becoming that I rest myself by stopping off at a psychological site where I can make a passage mine by dreaming it. Reading and rereading *The Lily in the Valley*, I have not managed to dominate my chagrin at seeing that Félix has left his river, "their river." Isn't the château of Clochegourde, surrounded by all of Touraine, enough to fortify Félix's *animus*? Couldn't Félix, a person with a weak childhood, more or less deprived of a mother, really become a man by living a faithful love? Yes, why has a great novel of reveries become a novel of social facts, and even historical facts? Such questions are all confessions of a reader who does not know how to read a book objectively, as if a book were a definitive object.

How can you be objective in the face of a book you love, which you have loved, which you have read at several different times in your life? Such a book has a *reading past*. In rereading it, you have not always suffered in the same way—and above all you no longer hope with the same intensity in all the seasons of a life of reading. Can one even relive the hopes of the first reading when he now knows that Félix will betray? The *animus* and *anima* quests do not yield the same riches at every age in the life of the reader. Above all the great books remain psychologically alive. You are never finished reading them.

VIII

The diagram we have indicated above is given by Jung in his work on the *Uebertragung*. In fact, Jung applies it there to the bonds between thought and reverie which are established between an alchemist and a female laboratory technician. The adept and the working girl form a double sign for telling the sexuality of the mysteries of the manipulated matter. We are going beyond the duality of the job and the household. In order to marry substances, one must have the double psychic magister of the adept's *animus* and the soror's *anima*. The "conjunction" of substances in alchemy is always a conjunction of the forces of the masculine and feminine principles. When these principles have been exalted, when they have received their total idealization, they are ready for the hierogamies.

In the hope of such unions, it is then a question, for the alchemist, of first breaking up the confused androgynies of natural substances and separating their solar and lunar forces, the active forces of fire and the accepting force of water. A reverie on the "purity" of substances—an almost moral purity—thus gives life to the long alchemical labors. Of course, this search for a purity which must reach to the very heart of substances has nothing in common with the preparation of pure compounds in modern chemistry. It does not involve the elimination of material impurities in a methodical job of fractional distillations. The absolute difference that exists between chemical and alchemical distillations will be immediately evident if we remember that, as soon as he has finished one distillation, the alchemist immediately starts the distillation anew, again mixing dead matter with the elixir, the pure with the impure, so that the elixir *learns*, as it were, to liberate itself from its soil. The scientist continues. The alchemist starts all over again. Thus, objective references to purifications of matter can teach us nothing about the reveries of purity which give the alchemist the patience to start over again. In alchemy we are not faced with intellectual patience, but we are within the very action of moral patience which searches out the impurities of a consciousness. *The alchemist is an educator of matter.*

And what a dream of primordial morality it would be if we could give their youth back to all the substances of the earth! After this long work of morality, the principles mixed in a primitive androgeneity are "purified" to the point of being worthy of a hierogamy. From androgeneity to hierogamy, such is the spread of alchemical meditations.

Very often, in the course of earlier works, we have insisted on the dominant psychological meanings of alchemical works. We allude to them here only to call to mind the existence of *elaborated reveries*. The alchemist's reveries want to be thoughts. For a long time, when we were attempting to write the history of these reveries, they crucified our mind in that torment of the false union of the concept and the image that we were talking about in the preceding chapter. In all the alchemist's works, the alchemist is looking for material verifications as if reverie were not sufficient unto itself. The *animus* thoughts want verifications in the *anima* reveries. The sense of this verification is the inverse of what could be desired by a scientific mind, a mind limited to its *animus* consciousness.

IX

In this digression, we have spread out into problems which take alchemical documents into account. The reason is that in them we find good examples of *complex* convictions, convictions which assemble syntheses of thoughts and conglomerates of images. Thanks to his complex convictions, made strong with the forces of *animus* and *anima*, the alchemist believes he is seizing the soul of the world, participating in the soul of the world. Thus, from the world to the man, alchemy is a problem of souls.

We ought to come upon the same problem in the reverie of union of two human souls, a reverie full of reversals which illustrate the theme: to conquer a soul is to find one's own soul. In the reveries of a lover, of a being dreaming of another being, the dreamer's *anima* deepens by dreaming the *anima* of the dreamed being. Here, the reverie of communion is no longer a philosophy of the communication of consciousnesses. It is life in a double, through a double, a life that takes on animation in an intimate dialectic of *animus* and *anima*. Doubling and splitting exchange functions. Doubling our being by idealizing the beloved being, we split our being into its two forces of *animus* and *anima*.

In order to measure all the idealizations of the being loved and adorned with virtues in a solitary reverie, in order to follow all the transpositions which give a psychological reality to idealities formulated by dreaming life, it is necessary, we believe, to envisage a *complex transfer* of a very different scope than the transfer encountered by psychoanalysts. While considering this complex transfer, we should recognize all the functions of the *Uebertragung* as Jung envisages it in his works on the psychology of alchemists. A simple translation of the word *Uebertragung* by the word "transfer," which was so widely used by classical psychoanalysts, simplifies problems too much. *Uebertragung* is, as it were, a transfer *over* the most contrasting characteristics. This transfer passes over the detail of everyday relationships, over social situations to link cosmic situations. One is then urged to understand man not only from the basis of his inclusion in the world but by following his impulses for idealization which are at work on the world.

To be convinced of the scope of this psychological explanation of man by the world worked on by androgynous reveries, it would be sufficient to meditate on the engravings in Jung's book[14]; as a matter of fact, Jung's book presents reproductions of a series of twelve engravings taken from an old book of alchemy, the *Rosarium Philosophorum*. These twelve engravings are all illustrations of the alchemical union of the King and Queen. This "King" and "Queen" reign in the same psychism; they are the majesties of the psychological forces which, thanks to the Work, are going to reign over things. The androgeneity of the dreamer proceeds to project itself in an androgeneity of the world. By following the twelve pictures in detail, by adding all the dialectics of the sun (*soleil*, m.) and the moon (*lune*, f.), of fire (*feu*, m.) and water (*eau*, f.), of the serpent (*serpent*, m.) and the dove (*colombe*, f.), short hair (*cheveux*, m.) and long hair (*chevelure*, f.), one recognizes the power of associated reveries which are also set under the sign of the adept and his female companion. There, two reveries of culture come into balance. We hold ourselves in an equilibrium of reverie by relying on the two crisscrossing transfers which follow the projections of the *animus* on the *anima* and of the *anima* on the *animus*.

In four of the twelve engravings from the *Rosarium Philosophorum* the union of the King and Queen is so complete that

---

14 C. G. Jung, *Die Psychologie der Uebertragung* (Zurich, 1946).

they no longer have but one single body. A single body dominated by two crowned heads. A beautiful symbol of the double
exaltation of androgeneity. Androgeneity is not buried away in
some indistinct bestiality at the obscure origins of life. It is a dialectic at the summit. Coming from one and the same being, it
shows the exaltation of the *animus* and the *anima*. It prepares the
associated reveries of the super-masculine and the super-feminine.

X

The support which we have just taken from a psychology of the
alchemist in order to sustain a philosophy of reverie can seem
very fragile and removed. It can also be objected that the traditional image of the alchemist is that of a solitary worker, an
image which could rightly be that of a philosopher who dreams in
his solitude. Isn't the metaphysician the alchemist with ideas too
big to be realized?

But are there objections capable of stopping a dreamer who
dreams on his reveries? I shall go to the bottom then of all the
paradoxes which give an intensity of being to ephemeral images.
Isn't this the first of the ontological paradoxes: by transporting
the dreamer into another world, reverie makes the dreamer into a
person different from himself. And yet this other person is still
himself, the double of himself. Literature on "the double" is not
lacking. Poets and writers can supply us with numerous documents. Psychologists and psychiatrists have studied the splitting
of the personality. But these "splittings" are extreme cases where,
in some way, the bonds between the two split personalities are
broken. Reverie—and not the dream—retains mastery over its
splittings. In the cases encountered in psychiatry, the profound
nature of reverie is obliterated. The "double" is often sustained
by an intellectuality; it records verifications which may be only
hallucinations. Sometimes writers themselves exaggerate. They
give body to phantasmagorical beings. They want to fascinate
us with extraordinary psychological exploits.

Just so many documents which are too big for us, just so many
experiences in which we are not participating. *Literary opium*
has never been able to make me dream.

So let us get back to simple reverie, to a reverie which can be ours. Often it is in some elsewhere, far from here, that reverie goes looking for our double. More often yet it is in a yesteryear which has disappeared forever. And then, after those splittings which are still related to our history, there is a splitting which, if one were "thinking," would be a philosopher's splitting: where am I? who am I? of what reflection of being am I the being? But these questions think too much. A philosopher would reinforce them with doubts. In reality, reverie splits the being more gently, more naturally. And with what variety! There are reveries where I am less than myself. Then the shadow is a rich being. It is a more penetrating psychologist than the psychologist of everyday life. This shadow knows the being which doubles the being of the dreamer through reverie. The shadow, the double of our being, knows the "psychology of the depths" in our reveries. And thus it is that the being projected by reverie—for our I-dreamer is a projected being—is double as we ourselves are, and is, like ourselves, *animus* and *anima*. Here we are at the knot of all our paradoxes: the *"double" is the double of a double being.*

Then, in the most solitary reveries, when we call forth vanished beings, when we idealize the persons who are dear to us, when in our readings we are free enough to live as man and woman, we feel that all of life takes on a double—that the past takes on a double, that all beings become double in their idealization, that the world incorporates all the beauties of our chimeras. Without chimeric psychology, there is no real psychology, no complete psychology. In his reveries, man is sovereign. In studying the real man, the psychology of observation only encounters an uncrowned being.

In order to analyze all the psychological potentialities offered to the solitary person in reverie, it will be necessary to start then from the motto: *I am alone, so there are four of us.* The solitary dreamer copes with quadripolar situations.[15]

I am alone so I dream of the being who had cured my solitude,

---

[15] Strindberg, it seems, knew this splitting of the double. He writes in *Légende:* "We begin to love a woman by depositing our soul near her, part by part. We split our person and the beloved woman who earlier was neutral and unimportant to us begins to don our other I; she becomes double." Quoted by Otto Rank, *Don Juan,* translation, p. 161 note.

who would have cured by solitudes. With its life, it brought me the idealizations of life, all the idealizations which give life a double, which lead life toward its summits, which make the dreamer too live by splitting, following the great motto of Patrice de La Tour du Pin who said that poets find "their base by ascending." [16]

When reverie has that kind of tonality, it is not a simple idealization of the beings of life. It is a psychological idealization in depth. It is a product (*oeuvre*) of creating (*créante*) psychology. Reverie brings to light an aesthetics of psychology. Reverie is then a product of creating psychology. And the idealized being starts talking with the idealizing being. He talks as a function of his own duality. A concert for four voices begins in the reverie of the solitary dreamer. For the double being he is in talking to his double, the dual language is not sufficient. A double dual, a "quadrial" language would be necessary. A linguist tells us there are languages which know this marvel without informing us very well about the dreaming people who speak it.[17]

And it is here that the intermediary play between thought and reverie, between the psychic functions of the real and the unreal multiplies and crisscrosses to produce the psychological marvels of human imagination. Man is an imagining being. For in the end, the irreality function functions as well in the face of man as in the face of the cosmos. What would we know of others if we did not imagine things? What psychological refinement don't we feel when we read a novelist who *invents man* and all the poets who invent the prestigious increments to the human dimension! And we live out these surpassings, without daring to speak them, in our taciturn reveries.

Ah! what a lot of undisciplined and indiscreet thoughts there are in the reveries of a man alone! What a company of dreamed beings there is in a solitary reverie!

And the being closest to us, our double—the double of our double being—in what crisscrossing projections it comes alive! And so it is, in our lucid reveries, that we know a sort of *interior transfer*, an *Uebertragung* which carries us beyond ourselves into

16 Patrice de La Tour du Pin, *La vie recluse en poésie*, p. 85.
17 Pierre Guiraud, *La grammaire*, "Que sais-je?," no. 788, p. 29.

another ourselves. Then the whole diagram we were proposing earlier to analyze interhuman relationships is valuable here, is useful here for analyzing our reveries as a solitary dreamer.

But let us go back a bit. Of course, in books of alchemy, there are numerous engravings which represent the adept and the soror standing before the athanor while a half-nude workman blows the fire in the bottom of the fire box with all his might. But is that really an image which describes a reality? The alchemist would have been extremely lucky if he had known a feminine companion in meditation, a soror of reveries. More likely he was alone, alone like all great dreamers. The image gives us a reverie situation. All the human supports, the soror who is meditating as well as the workman who is blowing the fire are imagined supports. The psychological unity of the tableau is obtained by criss-crossed transfers. All these transfers are interior, intimate. They yield relationships of a double to another intimate-double. The alchemist's confidence in his meditation and his works would come from the comfort lavished by his double's double. In the depths of his being, he was being helped by a soror. His *animus* at work was sustained by a transfiguration of his *anima*.

So when they are imagined, the ancient engravings and the ancient texts bring us, to some extent, evidence for a refined psychology. Alchemy is a nuanced materialism which one can understand only by participating in it with a feminine sensitivity, but by keeping a record, all the same, of all the little masculine rages with which the alchemist torments matter. The alchemist looks for the secret of the world the way a psychologist looks for the secret of a heart. And the soror is there to soften everything. At the bottom of every reverie, we find that being which deepens everything, a permanent being. For me, when the word *sister* comes up in the lines of a poet, I hear echoes of a distant alchemy. Is this a poetic text, or is it a text of the alchemy of the heart? Who is speaking in these two great lines?

> Come pray with me, my sister,
> To recover vegetable permanence.[18]

18 Edmond Vandercammen, *La porte sans mémoire*, p. 49.

"Vegetable permanence," what an *anima* truth, what a symbol for a soul's repose in a world worthy of dreams (*songes*)!

XI

By indicating—doubtless very imprudently—the paradox of our four-pole reveries, we have lost the support of the reveries of the poets which we habitually depend upon. On the other hand, if we had taken the liberty to look for references in scholarly books, we would not have had any difficulty outlining a philosophy of the androgynous being. Our only ambition is to draw attention to a poetics of the androgyny which would develop in the sense of a double idealization of the human element. In any event, one reads scholarly books concerning the androgyne differently, with a more profound sense of participation, if he has become conscious of the potentialities of *animus* and *anima* which reside at the bottom of every human soul. In correlation with this awareness in *animus* and *anima,* one could rid the myths of their overload of explicit historicity. Do we really need to have recourse to ante-human legends to participate in the androgyny when the psychism already bears such clear marks of an androgyny? Must we refer back to the Platonic culture of Schleiermacher, as Giese does in his fine book,[19] in order to grasp the dynamism of femininity of Plato's translator? Fritz Giese's book, parenthetically, is incomparably rich. In it, the social environment in which German Romanticism took form is presented within the great community of culture which united the thinkers with their female companions. It seems that in such a communion of hearts, it was the culture itself which was androgynous. Very often with German Romantic writers, reference to the *Symposium* is an oratorical precaution for dealing with an androgyny which is the very life of their poetic sensitivity. If the problem is posed on the single level of poetic creation, the habitual reference to temperaments seems to us to burden our research. The epithet *weiblich* (feminine) is a fallacious lable when attached to great creators. A psychism which opens up to the two potentialities of

---

[19] Fritz Giese, *Der romantische Charakter*, vol. I, 1919.

the *animus* and the *anima* escapes temperamental outbursts for
that very reason. At least that is our thesis and that is what justifies us, as we see it, in proposing a poetics of reverie as the doctrine of the constitution of a person (*être*)—a constitution of the
person which separates the person as *animus* (*être en animus*) on
the one hand from the person as *anima* on the other.

From then on, the androgyny is not behind us in some distant
organization of the biological being upon which a past of myths
and legends would comment; it is in front of us, open to every
dreamer who dreams of realizing the super-feminine as well as the
super-masculine. Reveries in *animus* and *anima* are thus psychologically prospective.

It must be clearly understood that the masculine and feminine
become *values* as soon as they are idealized. And reciprocally, if
they are not idealized, are they anything more than poor biological servitudes? It is then as values of poetic reverie, as principles
of idealizing reverie that a poetics of reverie must study the androgeneity designated by the *Animus-Anima* duality.

An emulation of being determines the values of the *more-
than-being*. A great line by Elizabeth Barrett Browning expands
all loving life: "Make thy love larger to enlarge my worth."

Such a line can be taken as the motto for a psychology of the
mutual idealization between two true lovers.

The intervention of a value completely changes the problem
posed by facts. Philosophy and religion can thus cooperate, as is
the case in the works of Soloview, to make the androgyny into the
basis for an anthropology. The documents which we would have
to work with come from a long meditation upon the Books of the
Apostles. We can not transfer them into a work which aims to deal
only with poetic values and simply at the level of the reverie of a
solitary dreamer. Let us note simply that the androgyne of Soloview is the creature (*être*) of a supraterrestrial destiny. This complete being appears in a will to the ideal which already inhabits
loving hearts, the most faithful followers of total love. Through a
great many sentimental failures, the great Russian philosopher
has preserved the heroism of pure love which prepares the androgynous life of the beyond. Metaphysical goals are so far from
our experience as a dreamer that we could have an inkling of

them only in a long study of the whole system. To prepare for such a study, the reader will be able to refer to Stremooukoff's thesis.[20] Let us simply keep in mind that for Soloview an exalted love must dominate life, lead life on toward its summit: "The veritable man in the plenitude of his ideal personality can not, obviously, be only man or woman, but must possess a superior unity of the two sexes. The realization of this unity, the creation of the veritable man—a free union of the masculine and feminine principles, maintaining their formal individualization, but having overcome their essential diversity and disintegration—that is precisely the proper and immediate task of love." [21]

By the very fact that we are limiting our efforts to bringing out the elements of a creating poetics, we can not take support from the numerous documents of philosophical anthropology. There are numerous pages in Koyré's thesis on Jacob Boehme and in Susini's thesis on Franz von Baader where man's veritable destiny is presented as a search for the lost androgeneity. For Baader, this recovered androgeneity would be a union at the summit in the complementarity of exalted values. After the fall, after the loss of the primitive androgeneity, Adam became the depository for "the severe force"; Eve "the guardian of tender softness." [22] Such values are hostile as long as they are separated. A reverie on human values must tend to coordinate them, must increase them in a reciprocal idealization. For a mystic like von Baader, this idealization is determined by religious meditation, but, itself separated from prayer, this idealization has a psychological existence. It is one of the dynamisms of reverie.

Naturally, a psychologist, even if he believes in its reality, will want to follow the integration of this idealization of masculine and feminine beings into practical life. Then the social marks of the masculine and the feminine will be determinant for him. The psychologist will always want to pass from images to the psychological reality. But our position as a phenomenologist simplifies the problem. By returning to the images of the masculine and the feminine—and even to the words which designate them—we are

20 D. Stremooukoff, *Vladimir Soloview et son oeuvre messianique* (Paris, 1935).
21 V. Soloview, *Le sense de l'amour*, translation, p. 59.
22 E. Susini, *Franz von Baader et le romantisme mystique*. Vrin, vol. II, p. 572.

returning to the idealizations as they really are. It will always be a fact that the woman is the person one idealizes, also the person who wishes his idealization. From the man to the woman and from the woman to the man, there is *anima* communication. In the *anima* there exists the common principle of the idealization of the human, the principle of the reverie of being, of a being which would want tranquility and, consequently, the continuity of being. Of course, the reverie of idealization is full of reminiscences. And so, in many respects, Jungian psychology is justified in seeing a process of projection in it. There exist numerous proofs that the lover does project maternal images upon the loved one. But all this material taken from an ancient, a very ancient past could easily mask the traits themselves of the idealization. The idealization can very well utilize "projections," but its movement is freer, goes farther, goes too far. All reality, that which is present, that which remains like the heritage of past time, is idealized, put into the movement of a dreamed reality.

But closer to the problems we are envisaging in this present book, there exists a great work where the psychology of *animus* and *anima* is presented as a veritable aesthetics of psychology. We are talking about Balzac's philosophical essay entitled *Séraphîta*. In many of its aspects, *Séraphîta* appears as a poem of the androgyny.

First, let us recall that the first chapter is entitled "Séraphîtüs," the second "Séraphîta" and the third "Séraphîta-Séraphîtüs." Thus, the *integral being,* the sum of the human, is presented successively in its active virtues of the masculine element, and in its conservative forces by the feminine before the synthesis is made as an entire solidarity between the *animus* and the *anima.* This synthesis gives rise to an assumption which bears the mark of what will be the supernatural destiny of Soloview's androgyne.

Opposite this androgynous being which dominates everything which is simply terrestrial in creation, Balzac put Minna, an innocent girl, and Wilfrid, a man who has known the passions of the city. Then the androgynous being is Séraphîtüs opposite Minna and Séraphîta opposite Wilfrid. Two unions could be made with the earth beings if the supraterrestrial being could divide and personify each of its forces socially, the virile ones and the feminine ones.

From then on, since there are two persons to love the androgyne in Balzac's philosophical novel, two persons to love the double being—since Séraphîtüs-Séraphîta alone possesses the double magnetism which attracts all dreams—there we are squarely in front of the four-pole reverie. Then what a lot of crisscrossed reveries there are in the pages of the great dreamer (*songeur*)! How well Balzac knows the double psychology of Her for Him and of Him for Her! When Minna loves Séraphîtüs, when Wilfrid loves Séraphîta, when Séraphîtüs-Séraphîta wants to elevate the two terrestrial passions to an idealized life, what a lot of "projections" there are of *animus* in *anima* and of *anima* in *animus*. Thus a poetry of the psychism of idealization, a psychological poetry of the exalted psychism is offered to us, the readers. And let no one try to tell us we are in total irreality. All these psychic tensions, all these illuminations of the being have been experienced in the soul-mind of the poet. In the background, down in the depths, way down in the depths, the novelist was well aware that human nature was weaving possibilities of union —a marriage perhaps—between Minna and Wilfrid.

In a household, dreams die out, forces run down, virtues become middle-class. And the *animus* and *anima* are manifest only too often in "animosity." Jung himself is well aware of this when he attacks—how far we are here from alchemical reveries!—the psychology of conjugal life in common: "The *anima* gives rise to illogical outbursts of temper; the *animus* produces irritating commonplaces." [23] Inconsistency or platitude, what a poor dialectic of everyday life! There, as Jung indicates, there is no longer anything but "parcellary personalities," personalities then which take on "the character of an inferior man or woman."

Such a novel of inferior natures was not what Balzac wanted to present to the Beloved, to "Mme Eveline de Hanska, née Countess Rzewuska" as the dedication to *Séraphîta* indicates.

In mediocre life, the designations as *animus* and *anima* are

---

[23] C. G. Jung, *Psychologie et religion*, translation, ed. Corréa, p. 54.

perhaps superfluous; simple designations as virile or effeminate can probably suffice. But if we are to understand the reveries of the being who loves, who would want to love, who regrets not being loved the way he loves—and Balzac was familiar with such reveries—the forces and virtues of the *anima* and the *animus* must be evoked in their idealization. The quadripolar reverie begins. The dreamer can easily project his own *anima* upon the image of the beloved. But in doing that, there is no simple egotism of the imagination. The dreamer wants his projected *anima* to have a personal *animus* as well, one which is not the simple reflection of his own *animus*. In his interpretation, the psychoanalyst is being too *passéiste*. The *anima* projected by the *animus* will have to be accompanied by an *animus* worthy of his partner's *animus*. It is then a complete double which is projected, a double with infinite kindness (*anima*) and great intelligence (*animus*). Nothing is forgotten in the processes of idealization. Reveries of idealization develop, not by letting oneself be taken in by memories, but by constantly dreaming the values of a being whom one would love. And that is the way a great dreamer dreams his double. His magnified double sustains him.

As for the end of the philosophical novel *Séraphîta*, the androgynous being, which condenses the supraterrestrial destinies of the feminine and the masculine, leaves the earth in an "assumption" in which a whole redeemed universe participates; the earthly beings, Wilfrid and Minna, remain dynamized by a destiny of idealization. The dominant lesson of Balzac's meditation is the incorporation of an ideal of life in life itself. The reverie which idealizes the relationships of *animus* and *anima* is then an integral part of real life; reverie is an active force in the destiny of persons who wish to unite their life through a growing love. Psychological complexities are harmonized by the ideal. Those are themes which parcellizing psychology—the one which wears itself out looking for a nucleus of being—can scarcely envisage. And yet, a book is a human fact; a great book like *Séraphîta* gathers together numerous psychological elements. These elements become coherent through a sort of psychological beauty. It does the reader a service. For the person who likes to dream within the system of the *animus* and *anima*, reading this book is like an expansion of the being. For the person who likes to lose himself in the forest of the *anima,* reading this book is a deepening of the being. To such a dreamer, it seems that the world must be redeemed by the feminine being.

Reading the book of a great dreamer this way, in full reverie, one is astonished by a reader who is not astonished when confronted with an astonishing book. Hippolyte Taine opened his eyes very wide and was incapable of seeing anything. Doesn't he say, after reading *Séraphîta* and *Louis Lambert* which he calls "legitimate or adulterous children of philosophy": "Many people tire of them and reject *Séraphîta* and *Louis Lambert* as hollow dreams which are hard to read." [24]

What better way is there to convince oneself that a great book must be read twice than to be faced with such a judgment? It must be read once while "thinking" as Taine does, and once while dreaming in the company of reverie with the dreamer who wrote it.[25]

XII

At the time of German Romanticism, when people were trying to explain the nature of man with the aid of new scientific knowledge of physical and chemical phenomena, they did not hesitate to relate the difference between the sexes with the polarity of electric phenomena and also with the still more mysterious polarity of magnetism. Didn't Goethe say: "Das Magnet ist ein Urphänomen"—"The magnet is a basic phenomenon." And Goethe continued: "A basic phenomenon which is sufficiently explained by being expressed; thus it becomes a symbol for all other phenomena." [26] So people were basing themselves on a naive physics in order to explain a rich psychology of observations by the great observers of human nature. A genius of thought like Goethe, a genius of reverie like Franz von Baader descend that slope where the explanation forgets the nature of what must be explained.

Contemporary psychology, enriched by the diverse schools of

---

[24] H. Taine, *Nouveaux essais de critique et d'histoire,* 9th edition, 1914, p. 90.
[25] We take the liberty to refer the reader to the preface we wrote to *Séraphîta* in the edition of the complete works of Balzac, *Formes et reflets,* 1952, vol. 12.
[26] Quoted by Fritz Giese, *Der romantische Charakter,* 1919, vol. I, p. 298.

psychoanalysis and psychology of the depths, must reverse the perspective of such explanations. Psychology must develop autonomous explanations. Besides, the progress of scientific knowledge destroys even the framework of the old explanations which defined the cosmic characteristics of human nature too superficially. The steel magnet which attracts the soft iron, as people like Goethe, Schelling and Ritter contemplated it, is only a plaything, an outmoded plaything. In the most elementary scientific culture of our day, the magnet is no longer the pretext for anything more than a beginning lesson. The physics of physicians and mathematicians makes a homogeneous doctrine out of electromagnetism. In such a doctrine one would no longer find the least trace of reveries which could lead us from magnetic polarity to the polarity of masculine and feminine genders.

We are making this remark to accentuate the separation—which we were positing as necessary at the end of the preceding chapter—between the rationalism of scientific thought and a philosophical meditation on the aestheticizing values of human nature.

But once all reference to physical polarities has been pushed aside, the problem of psychological polarity which preoccupied the Romantics so much remains. The human being taken in his profound reality as well as in his great tension of becoming is a divided being, a being which divides again, having permitted himself the illusion of unity for barely an instant. He divides and then reunites. On the theme of *animus* and *anima,* if he were to go to the extremes of division, he would become a grimace of the man. Such grimaces exist: there are men and women who are too male—there are men and women who are too female. Nature in its goodness tends to eliminate these excesses to the benefit of an intimate commerce of the forces of *animus* and *anima* in one and the same soul.

Of course, the phenomena of polarity which the psychology of the depths designates by the *animus-anima* dialectic are complex. A philosopher who is far removed from precise physiological knowledge is not well prepared to measure well defined organic causalities in the psychism. But he is tempted to break with the physiological realities as he has broken with the physical realities.

In any event, one aspect of the problem does lie within his domain: that of the idealizing polarities. If one pushes the dreaming philosopher to polemics, he will declare that the idealizing values do not have any cause. Idealization does not belong to the realm of causality.

Let us recall then that, in this book, we are setting ourselves the precise task of studying the idealizing reverie, a reverie which places a dreamed communion of *animus* and *anima,* the two principles of the integral being, in the soul of a dreamer of human values.

For such studies of the idealizing reverie, the philosopher is no longer limited to his own dreams. Precisely, the whole of Romanticism, once rid of its occultism, its magic and its heavy cosmicity, can be relived as a humanism of idealized love. If one could also detach it from its history, if one could grasp it in its abundant life and transport it into an idealized life in the present, he would recognize that it retains an ever available psychic action. The very rich and profound passages which Wilhelm von Humboldt devotes to the problems of the difference between genders emphasizes a difference between the masculine and feminine geniuses. They help us define beings by their summits.[27] And that is thus that Wilhelm von Humboldt would have us grasp the profound action of the masculine and feminine genders upon works of art. In our reader reveries, we must accept the masculine or feminine partialities of the writer. As soon as it is a question of the man who is producing the poetic works, there is no *neuter gender.*

Doubtless, by reading Romantic texts as a dreamer, with their actuality restored by reverie, we take pleasure in a utopia of reading. We are treating literature as an absolute value. We are detaching the literary act, not only from its historical context, but also from its context in current psychology. For us, a book is always an emergence above everyday life. A book is expressed life and thus is an addition to life.

In our utopia of reading, we thus abandon the worries of the biographer's trade, the customary determinations of the psycholo-

[27] Cf. Wilhelm von Humboldt Werke, edit. Leitzmann, 1903, vol. I: *Ueber den Geschlechtsunterschied und dessen Einflusz auf die organische Natur* (1794), i. 311.

gist, determinations necessarily formulated on the man in the street. And naturally we do not believe it is useful, in connection with the problems of idealization in *animus* and *anima*, to bring up physiological aspects. The works are there to justify our inquiries into ideality. A hormone explanation of *Séraphitüs-Séraphita* or of *Pelléas and Mélisande* would be buffoonery. So we have the right to consider poetic works as effective human realities. In those which we have mentioned, there is the realization of an effective idealization in *animus* and *anima*.

The idealizing reverie goes in just one direction, from level to ever more elevated level. A reader who does not follow the ascension closely may have the impression that the work is fleeing away from him in evanescense. But the person who dreams better teaches himself to repress nothing. The reveries of excessive idealization are liberated from all repression. When they have taken flight, they have "passed beyond the wall of the psychoanalysts."

The excessive reverie, the idealizing reverie reaching depths as complex as those of the relationships between virility and femininity reveals itself as an exploit of the imagined life. This life imagined in a reverie which fills a dreamer with its gifts is elaborated to the benefit of his *anima*. The *anima* is always the refuge of the simple, tranquil, continuous life. Jung was able to say: "I have defined the *anima* very simply as the Archetype of life." [28] It is the Archetype of the immobile, stable, harmonious life well accorded to the fundamental rhythms of an existence devoid of drama. Whoever dreams (*songe*) of life, of the simple life without looking for knowledge (*savoir*) inclines toward the feminine. By being concentrated around the *anima*, reveries help the dreamer find his repose. In each of us, man or woman, the best of our reveries come from our feminine element. They bear the mark of an undeniable femininity. If we did not have a feminine being within us, how would we rest ourselves?

That is why we have believed we could inscribe all of our reveries on Reverie under the sign of the *Anima*.

---

[28] C. G. Jung, *Métamorphoses de l'âme et ses symboles*, translated by Le Lay. (Geneva, 1953) Georg, p. 72.

XIII

For those of us who can only work on written documents, on documents which are produced by a will to "edit," a certain indecision cannot be obliterated in the conclusions which terminate our inquiries. In point of fact, who writes? The *animus* or the *anima*? Is it possible for a writer to carry his *animus* sincerity and his *anima* sincerity through to the very end? We are not as confident as the annotater of Eckermann's book who was to take the following statement as an axiom for determining a psychology of the writer: "Tell me whom you create and I shall tell you who you are." [29] The literary creation of a woman by a man or of a man by a woman are burning creations. We would have to interrogate the creator with a double question: what are you in *animus?*—what are you in *anima?* And immediately the literary work, the literary creation would enter into the worst ambiguities. By following the simplest axis of happy reverie, we take pleasure in reveries of idealization. But in the will to create beings which the writer wishes to be real, hard, virile, reverie fades into the background. And the writer accepts a perspective of debasement. Compensations come into play. An *animus* which has not found a pure enough *anima* in life comes to despise the feminine. In the psychologically real, he would wish to find the roots of idealization. He is rebellious to the idealization which is, however, at its roots, in his own being.

As for us, we shall forbid ourselves to cross the barrier, to go from the psychology of the work to the psychology of its author. I shall never be anything but a psychologist of books. In this psychology of books, at least two hypotheses must be tested: the man resembles the work; the man is different from the work. And why wouldn't the two hypotheses, taken together, be valid? One contradiction more or less will not matter to psychology. By measuring the extent to which these two hypotheses are applicable, one can study the psychology of compensation in all its subtleties, in all its subterfuges.

In the extreme case of the contradictions of *animus* and *anima*

[29] *Conversations de Goethe recueillies par Eckermann*, translated by Emile Délérot, 1883, vol. I, p. 88.

which appear in works that "contradict" their authors, the causality of heavy passions must be abandoned. In 1891, Valéry wrote
to Gide: "When Lamartine wrote *The Fall of an Angel*, all the
women of Paris were his mistresses. When Rachilde wrote *Monsieur Vénus*, she was a virgin." [30]

What psychoanalyst will help us enter all the twists and de-
tours of the preface Maurice Barrès wrote in 1889 for Rachilde's
book *Monsieur Vénus?* This preface is appropriately entitled
"The Complications of Love." How astonishing this book was for
Barrès, "this erudite vice bursting forth in the dream of a virgin."
"Rachilde was somehow born with an infamous and coquettish
mind." And quoting Rachilde, Barrès continues: "God should
have created love on one side and the senses on the other. True
love should never be composed of anything but warm friendship." [31]

And Maurice Barrès concludes: "Doesn't it seem to us that
Monsieur Vénus, over and above the light it sheds on a certain
depravity of our time, is an infinitely arresting case for those who
are preoccupied with the relationships which unite the work of
art to the brain which set it up and which are so difficult to
grasp?" [32]

To idealize the woman well, it will always be true that one
must be a man, a dream man (*homme de songe*) comforted by his
consciousness as *anima*. After the first passions, doesn't Barrès
dream of "creating himself a fine, gentle feminine image which
would throb within him, which would be him." [33] In a veritable
declaration to his *anima,* he manages to say: "And it is I alone
whom I love for the feminine perfume of my soul." In this statement, Barrès' egotism takes on a dialectic which can be analyzed
only in a psychology of *animus* and *anima*. At the beginning of
the account, it was possible to read that it was a question not of a
love story, but rather of "the history of a soul with its two elements, feminine and male." [34]

---

[30] Quoted by Henri Mondor, *Les premiers temps d'une amitié*, p. 146.
[31] Rachilde, *Monsieur Vénus,* Preface by Maurice Barrès. (Paris, 1889) Félix
Brossier, p. xvii.
[32] *Loc. cit.,* p. xxi.
[33] Maurice Barrès, *Sous l'oeil des barbares,* ed. Emile Paul, 1911, pp. 115, 117.
[34] *Loc. cit.,* p. 57.

Doubtless, the dreamer is off to a bad start if he wants to go from Bérénice to Beatrice, from Barrès' account of wretched sensuality to the greatest idealizations of human values in Dante. It seems striking to us at least, that Barrès himself looked for this idealization. He knew the problem posed by Dante's philosophy; doesn't Beatrice represent Woman, the Church, Theology? Beatrice is a synthesis of the greatest idealizations: for a dreamer of human values, she is the erudite *Anima*. She radiates by the heart and the intelligence. A great book would be necessary to deal with this problem. But this book has been written. The reader can refer to Etienne Gilson's work, *Dante and Philosophy*.[85]

---

[85] E. Gilson, *Dante et la philosophie*, (Paris, 1939) Vrin.

Three

Reveries toward Childhood

Solitude, my mother, tell me my life again.
> O. V. de Milosz,
> *Symphonie de septembre*

> To some extent, I have only lived to have some-
> thing to outlive. By confiding these futile re-
> membrances to paper, I am conscious of accom-
> plishing the most important act of my life. I was
> predestined to Memory.
>> O. V. de Milosz,
>> *L'amoureuse initiation*

I bring you some water lost in your memory—
follow me to the spring and find its secret.
> Patrice de la Tour du Pin,
> *Le second jeu*

I

When, all alone and dreaming on rather at length, we go far from the present to relive the times of the first life, several child faces come to meet us. We were several in the trial life (*la vie essayée*), in our primitive life. Only through the accounts of others have we come to know of our unity. On the thread of our history as told by the others, year by year, we end up resembling ourselves. We gather all our beings around the unity of our name.

But reverie does not recount. Or at least there are reveries so deep, reveries which help us descend so deeply within ourselves that they rid us of our history. They liberate us from our name. These solitudes of today return us to the original solitudes. Those original solitudes, the childhood solitudes leave indelible marks on certain souls. Their entire life is sensitized for poetic reverie, for a reverie which knows the price of solitude. Childhood knows unhappiness through men. In solitude, it can relax its aches. When the human world leaves him in peace, the child feels like the son of the cosmos. And thus, in his solitudes, from the moment he is master of his reveries, the child knows the happiness of dreaming which will later be the happiness of the poets. How is it possible not to feel that there is communication between our solitude as a dreamer and the solitudes of childhood? And it is no accident that, in a tranquil reverie, we often follow the slope which returns us to our childhood solitudes.

Let us leave to psychoanalysis then the task of curing badly spent childhoods, of curing the puerile sufferings of an *indurate childhood* which oppresses the psyche of so many adults. There is a task open to a poetico-analysis which would help us reconstitute within ourselves the being of liberating solitudes. Poetico-analysis ought to return all the privileges of the imagination to us. Memory is a field full of psychological ruins, a whatnot full of memories. Our whole childhood remains to be reimagined. In reimagining it, we have the possibility of recovering it in the very life of our reveries as a solitary child.

From then on, the theses which we wish to defend in this chapter all return to make us recognize within the human soul the permanence of a nucleus of childhood, an immobile but ever living childhood, outside history, hidden from the others, disguised in history when it is recounted, but which has real being only in its instants of illumination which is the same as saying in the moments of its poetic existence.

When he would dream in his solitude, the child knew an existence without bounds. His reverie was not simply a reverie of escape. It was a reverie of flight.

There are childhood reveries which surge forth with the brilliance of a fire. The poet finds his childhood again by telling it with a tone (*verbe*) of fire.

> Tone on fire. I shall tell what my childhood was.
> We unearthed the red moon in the thick of the woods.[1]

An excess of childhood is the germ of a poem. One would laugh at a father who, for love of his child, would go "unhook the moon." But the poet does not shy away from this cosmic gesture. In his ardent memory, he knows that that is a childhood gesture. The child knows very well that the moon, that great blond bird, has its nest somewhere in the forest.

Thus, childhood images, images which a child could make, images which a poet tells us that a child has made are, for us, manifestations of the permanent childhood. Those are the images of solitude. They tell of the continuity of the great childhood reveries with the reveries of the poet.

---

[1] Alain Bosquet, *Premier testament*, Paris, Gallimard, p. 17.

II

So it seems that, with the aid of the poet's images, childhood will be revealed as psychologically beautiful. How can we avoid speaking of psychological beauty when confronted with an attractive event from our inner life. This beauty is within us, at the bottom of memory. It is the beauty of a flight which revives us, which puts the dynamism of one of life's beauties within us. In our childhood, reverie gave us freedom. It is striking that the most favorable field for receiving the consciousness of freedom is none other than reverie. To grasp this liberty when it intervenes in a child's reverie is paradoxical only if one forgets that we still dream of liberty as we dreamed of it when we were children. What other psychological freedom do we have than the freedom to dream? Psychologically speaking, it is in reverie that we are free beings.

A potential childhood is within us. When we go looking for it in our reveries, we relive it even more in its possibilities than in its reality.

We dream of everything that it could have been; we dream at the frontier between history and legend. To reach the memories of our solitudes, we idealize the worlds in which we were solitary children. So it is a problem in practical psychology to take into account the very real idealization of childhood memories and the personal interest we take in all childhood memories. And for that reason there is communication between a poet of childhood and his reader through the intermediary of the childhood which endures within us. Furthermore, this childhood continues to be receptive to any opening upon life and makes it possible for us to understand and love children as if we were their equals in original life.

A poet speaks to us and we are a living water, a new wellspring. Let us listen to Charles Plisnier:

> Ah, provided I consent to it
> my childhood there you are
> as alive, as present

> Firmament of blue glass
> tree of leaf and snow
> river that runs, where am I going? [2]

Reading these lines I see the blue sky above my river in the summers of the other century.

The being of reverie crosses all the ages of man from childhood to old age without growing old. And that is why one feels a sort of redoubling of reverie late in life when he tries to bring the reveries of childhood back to life.

This reinforcement of reverie, this deepening of reverie which we feel when we dream of our childhood explains that, in all reverie, even that which takes us into the contemplation of a great beauty of the world, we soon find ourselves on the slope of memories; imperceptibly, we are being led back to old reveries, suddenly so old that we no longer think of dating them. A glimmer of eternity descends upon the beauty of the world. We are standing before a great lake whose name is familiar to geographers, high in the mountains, and suddenly we are returning to a distant past. We dream while remembering. We remember while dreaming. Our memories bring us back to a simple river which reflects a sky leaning upon hills. But the hill gets bigger and the loop of the river broadens. The little becomes big. The world of childhood reverie is as big, bigger than the world offered to today's reverie. From poetic reverie, inspired by some great spectacle of the world to childhood reverie, there is a commerce of grandeur. And that is why childhood is at the origin of the greatest landscapes. Our childhood solitudes have given us the primitive immensities.

By dreaming on childhood, we return to the lair of reveries, to the reveries which have opened up the world to us. It is reverie which makes us the first inhabitant of the world of solitude. And we inhabit the world better because we inhabit it as the solitary child inhabits images. In the child's reverie, the image takes precedent over everything else. Experiences come only later. They go against the wind of every reverie of flight. The child sees every-

---

2 Charles Plisnier, *Sacre*, XXI.

thing big and beautiful. The reverie toward childhood returns us to the beauty of the first images.

Can the world be as beautiful now? Our adherence to the original beauty was so strong that if our reverie carries us back to our dearest memories, the present world is completely colorless. A poet who writes a book of poems entitled *Concrete Days* can say:

> . . . The world totters
> when from my past I get
> what I need to live in the depths of myself.[3]

Ah! how solid we would be within ourselves if we could live, live again without nostalgia and in complete ardor, in our primitive world.

In short, isn't that opening on the world of which philosophers avail themselves, a reopening upon the prestigious world of original contemplations? But put another way, is this intuition of the world, this *Weltanschauung* anything other than a childhood which dares not speak its name? The roots of the grandeur of the world plunge into a childhood. For man, the world begins with a revolution of the soul which very often goes back to a childhood. A passage by Villiers de L'Isle-Adam will give us an example of this. In 1862 in his book *Isis,* he wrote of his heroine, the dominating woman: "The character of her mind was self-determining, and by obscure transitions it attained the immanent proportions where the self is affirmed for what it is. The nameless hour, the eternal hour when children cease to look vaguely at the sky and the earth rang for her in her ninth year. From this moment on, what was dreaming confusedly in the eyes of this little girl took on a more fixed glint: one would have said she was feeling the meaning of herself while awakening in our shadows."[4]

Thus, in "a nameless hour," "the world is affirmed for what it is," and the soul which dreams is a consciousness of solitude. At the end of Villiers de L'Isle-Adam's account (p. 225), the heroine will be able to say: "My memory, suddenly damaged in the deep

---

[3] Paul Chaulot, *Jours de béton*, edit. Amis de Rochefort, p. 98.
[4] Count of Villiers de L'Isle-Adam, *Isis*. (Brussels and Paris, 1862) Librairie Internationale, p. 85.

domains of the dream, felt inconceivable memories." Thus, the soul and the world are both open to the immemorial.

So, like a forgotten fire, a childhood can always flare up again within us. The fire of yesteryear and the cold of today meet in a great poem by Vincent Huidobro:

> In my childhood is born a childhood burning like alcohol
> I would sit down in the paths of the night
> I would listen to the discourse of the stars
> And that of the tree.
> Now indifference snows in the evening of my soul.[5]

These images which arise from the depths of childhood are not really memories. In order to evaluate all their vitality, a philosopher would have to be able to develop all the dialectics that are summed up too quickly in the two words "imagination" and "memory." We are going to devote a short paragraph to pointing up the boundaries between memories and images.

III

When we were gathering together the themes which constituted, in our eyes, the "psychology" of the house for our book *The Poetics of Space*, we saw the endless play of the dialectics of facts and values, realities and dreams, memories and legends, projects and chimeras. Examined within such dialectics, the past is not stable; it does not return to the memory either with the same traits or in the same light. As soon as the past is situated within a net work of human values, within the inner values of a person who does not forget, it appears with the double force of the mind which remembers and the soul which feasts upon its faithfulness. The soul and the mind do not have the same memory. Sully Prudhomme, who has experienced this division, wrote:

> O memory, the soul renounces,
> Frightened, to conceive you.

It is only when the soul and the mind are united in a reverie by the reverie that we benefit from the union of imagination and

---

[5] Vincent Huidobro, *Altaible*, translated by Vincent Verhesen, p. 56.

memory. In such a union we can say that we are reliving our past. Our past being imagines itself living again.

From then on, in order to constitute the poetics of a childhood set forth in a reverie, it is necessary to give memories their atmosphere of images. In order to make our philosopher's reflections on remembering reverie clearer, let us distinguish a few polemical points between psychological facts and values.

In their psychic primitiveness, Imagination and Memory appear in an indissoluble complex. If they are attached to perception, they are being badly analyzed. The remembered past is not simply a past of perception. Since one is remembering, the past is already being designated in a reverie as an image value. From their very origin, the imagination colors the paintings it will want to see again. For facts to go as far as the archives of the memory, values must be rediscovered beyond the facts. Familiarity is not analyzed by counting repetitions. The techniques of experimental psychology can scarcely hope to undertake a study of the imagination from the point of view of its creative values. In order to relive the *values of the past,* one must dream, must accept the great dilation of the psyche known as reverie, in the peace of a great repose. Then Memory and Imagination rival each other in giving us back the images which pertain to our lives.

In brief, it is the task of the *animus'* memory to tell the facts well in the objectivity of a life's history. But the *animus* is the outside man, the man who needs others in order to think. Who will help us to find the world of the intimate psychological values which is within us? The more I read poets, the more comfort and peace I find in the reveries of memory. Poets help us cherish our *anima* happinesses. Naturally, the poet tells us nothing of our objective past. But by the quality of the imagined life, the poet places a new light within us; in our reveries we paint impressionistic pictures of our past. Poets convince us that all our childhood reveries are worth starting over again.

The triple liaison between imagination, memory and poetry will then have to help us situate—and this is the second theme of our research—that human phenomenon which is a solitary childhood, a cosmic childhood, within the realm of values. If we could develop our outline, it would then be, for us, a matter of awakening within us, through a reading of the poets, and sometimes thanks to nothing more than a poet's image, a state of new childhood, of a childhood which goes farther than the memories of our childhood, as if the poet were making us continue, complete a childhood which was not well finished (accomplie), and yet which was ours and which we have doubtless dreamed on many occasions. The poetic documents we shall gather together ought then to return us to the natural, original oneirism which has no preconditions, the very oneirism of our childhood reveries.

These childhoods multiplied in a thousand images are certainly not dated. It would be going against their oneirism to try to fit them into coincidences in order to link them to the little facts of domestic life. Reverie shifts blocks of thoughts without any great worry about following the thread of an adventure. In that it is much different from the dream which always wants to tell us a story.

The history of our childhood is not psychically dated. Dates are put back in afterwards; they come from other people, from elsewhere, from another time than the time lived. Dates come from precisely that time when one is *recounting*. Victor Ségalen, a great dreamer of life, felt the difference between the recounted childhood and the childhood replaced in a dreamed duration: "One tells a child of some trait of his early childhood; he retains it, and will make use of it later in order to remember, and in turn recite and prolong, through repetition, the artificial duration." [6] And in another passage,[7] Victor Ségalen intends to rediscover "the early adolescent" and really meet "for the first time" with the adolescent he was. If memories are too often repeated, "that rare phantom" is no longer anything but a lifeless copy. The "pure memories" endlessly repeated become old refrains of the personality.

How often can a "pure memory" warm a remembering soul? Can't the "pure memory" too become a habit? In enriching our monotonous reveries, in revitalizing the "pure memories" which repeat themselves, we receive great help from the "variations"

---

6 Victor Ségalen, *Voyage au pays du réel.* (Paris, 1929) Plon, p. 214.
7 *Loc. cit.*, p. 222.

offered to us by the poets. The psychology of the imagination must be a doctrine of "psychological variations." The imagination is so current a faculty that it stimulates "variations" even in our memories of childhood. All these poetic variations which come to us in exaltation are just so many proofs of the permanence within us of a nucleus of childhood. If we wish to grasp its essence as a phenomenologist, history hampers us more than it helps us.

Such a phenomenological project of gathering the poetry of childhood reveries in its personal actuality is naturally much different from the very useful objective examinations of the child by psychologists. Even by letting children speak freely, by observing them uncensured while they are enjoying the total liberty of their play, by listening to them with the gentle patience of a child psychoanalyst, one does not necessarily attain the simple purity of phenomenological examination. People are much too well educated for that and consequently too disposed to apply the comparative method. A mother who sees her child as someone *incomparable* would know better. But alas! a mother does not know for very long . . . From the time a child reaches the "age of reason," from the time he loses his absolute right to imagine the world, his mother, like all educators, makes it her duty to teach him to be *objective*—objective in the simple way adults believe themselves to be "objective." He is stuffed with sociability. He is prepared for his life as a man along the lines of the ideal of stabilized men. He is also instructed in the history of his family. He is taught most of the memories of early childhood, a whole history which the child will always be able to recount. Childhood—that dough! —is pushed into the die so that the child will follow closely in the path of the lives of others.

The child thus enters into the zone of family, social and psychological conflicts. He becomes a premature man. This is the same as saying that this premature man is in a state of repressed childhood.

The questioned child, the child examined by the adult psychologist, who is strong in his consciousness as *animus,* does not surrender his solitude. The solitude of the child is more secret than the solitude of a man. It is often late in life that we discover

our childhood and adolescent solitudes in their depths. In the last
quarter of life one understands the solitudes of the first quarter
by reflecting the solitude of old age off the forgotten solitudes of
childhood.[8] The child dreamer is alone, very much alone. He
lives in the world of his reverie. His solitude is less social, less
pitted against society, than the solitude of men. The child knows
a natural reverie of solitude, a reverie which must not be confused with that of the sulking child. In his happy solitudes, the
dreaming child knows the cosmic reverie which unites us to the
world.

In our opinion, it is in the memories of this cosmic solitude
that we ought to find the nucleus of childhood which remains at
the center of the human psyche. It is there that imagination and
memory are most closely bound together. It is there that the
being of childhood binds the real with the imaginary, that it lives
the images of reality in total imagination. And all these images of
its cosmic solitude react in depth in the being of the child; aside
from his being for men, a being for the world is created under the
inspiration of the world. That is the being of cosmic childhood.
Men pass; the cosmos remains, an ever primitive cosmos, a cosmos
that the world's greatest spectacles will not erase in the entire
course of life. The cosmicity of our childhood remains within us.
In solitude, it reappears in our reveries. This nucleus of cosmic
childhood is then like a false memory within us. Our solitary reveries are the activities of a meta-amnesia. It seems that our reveries toward the reveries of our childhood introduce us to a being
preconditional to our being, a whole perspective on the *antecedence of being.*

---

[8] Gerard de Nerval writes: "The memories of childhood come back to life
when one reaches the halfway point in life" (*Les filles du feu, Angélique,* 6th
letter, ed. du Divan, p. 80). Our childhood waits a long time before being re-
integrated into our life. This reintegration is doubtless possible only in the
last half of life when one goes back down the hill. Jung writes (*Die Psychologie der Uebertragung,* p. 167): "The integration of the Self, taken in its profound sense, is a matter for the second half of life." As long as one is in the
bloom of life, it seems that the adolescence which survives within us puts up
a barrier to the childhood which is waiting to be relived. This childhood is
the reign of the self, of the *Selbst* set forth by Jung. Psychoanalysis should be
practiced by old men.

Were we or were we dreaming of being, and now in dreaming on our childhood, are we ourselves?

The antecedence of being is lost in the distance of time, that is, in the distances of our intimate time, in that multiple indetermination of our births to the psychism, for the psychism is tried out in many trials. The psychism is endlessly striving to be born. This antecedence of being and the infinity of the time of slow childhood are correlative. History—always the history of others!—caked onto the limbo of the psychism obscures all the forces of the personal meta-amnesia. And yet, psychologically speaking, *limbo* is not a *myth*. It is an indelible psychic reality. And to help us penetrate into the limbo of the antecedence of being, a few rare poets will supply us with rays of light. Rays? Limitless light! Edmond Vandercammen writes:

> Ever upstream from myself
> I advance, implore and pursue myself
> —O harsh law of my poem
> In the hollow of a shadow which flees me.[9]

In quest of the most distant memory, the poet wants a viaticum, a first value greater than the simple memory of an event from his history:

> Where I thought I was remembering
> I wanted only a little salt
> To recognize myself and be on my way.

And in another poem going upstream from upstream, the poet can say: "Aren't our years mineral dreams?" [10]

If the senses remember, aren't they going to find, within some archaeology of the perceptible, these "mineral dreams," these dreams of the "elements," which attach us to the world in an "eternal childhood."

"Upstream from myself," says the poet; "Upstream from upstream," says the reverie which looks to go back up to the springs (*sources*) of the being; those are the proofs of the antecedence of

---

[9] Edmond Vandercammen, *La porte sans mémoire*, p. 15.
[10] E. Vandercammen, *loc. cit.*, p. 39.

being. Poets look for this antecedence of being; therefore it exists. Such a certainty is one of the axioms of a philosophy of the oneirism.

In what beyond are poets not capable of remembering? Isn't early life a trial for eternity? Jean Follain can write:

> While in the fields
> of his eternal childhood
> the poet walks
> and doesn't want to forget anything.[11]

How vast life is when one meditates upon its beginnings! Isn't meditating upon an origin dreaming? And isn't dreaming upon an origin going beyond it? Beyond our history extends "our incommensurable memory" to take an expression which Baudelaire borrowed from de Quincey.[12]

In order to force the past, when forgetfulness is hemming us in, poets engage us in reimagining the lost childhood. They teach us "the audacities of the memory." [13] One poet tells us the past must be invented:

> Invent. There is no lost feast
> At the bottom of memory.[14]

And when the poet invents those great images which reveal the intimacy of the world, isn't he remembering?

Sometimes adolescence upsets everything. Adolescence, that fever of time in the human life! The memories are too clear for the dreams to be great. And the dreamer knows very well that he must go beyond the time of fevers to find the tranquil time, the time of the happy childhood inside his own substance. What sensitivity to the boundary between the times of tranquil childhood and the times of agitated adolescence there is in this passage by Jean Follain: "There were mornings when it rained substance. . . . That feeling of eternity which very early childhood carries

---

11 Jean Follain, *Exister*, p. 37.
12 Baudelaire, *Les paradis artificiels*, p. 329.
13 Pierre Emmanuel, *Tombeau d'Orphée*, p. 49.
14 Robert Ganzo, *L'oeuvre poétique*, Grasset, p. 46.

with it had already disappeared." [15] What a change there is in life
when on falls under the reign of the time which consumes, of the
time when the substance of the being has tears!

One has but to meditate on all the poems we have just quoted.
They are very different and yet they all bear witness to an aspira-
tion to cross the line, to go against the current, to rediscover the
great calm lake where time rests from its flowing. And this lake is
within us, like a primitive water, like the environment in which
an immobile childhood continues to reside.

When the poets call us toward this region, we know a tender
reverie, a reverie hypnotized by the faraway. It is this tension of
childhood reveries which we designate, for lack of a better name,
by the term "antecedence of being." To catch a glimpse of it, it is
necessary to take advantage of the *detemporalization* of the
states of great reverie. Thus we believe that one can know states
which are ontologically below being and above nothingness. In
these states the contradiction between being and non-being fades
away. A sub-being (*moins-être*) is trying itself out as being. This
antecedence of being does not yet have the responsibility of
being. Neither does it have the solidity of the constituted being
which believes itself capable of confronting a non-being. In such
a state of mind, one feels clearly that logical opposition, with its
too bright light, erases all possibility of penumbral ontology.
Very much softened keys are necessary to follow, in a dialectic of
light and shadow, all the emergences of the human trying itself
out at being.

The terms "life" and "death" are too approximate. In a reverie, the word "death" is vulgar. It ought not to be used in a
micrometaphysical study of the being which appears and disappears only to reappear, following the undulations of a reverie on
being. Besides, if one dies in certain dreams, in reveries or, in
other words, in the peaceful oneirism, one does not die. Is it necessary to add that, in a general manner, birth and death are not
psychologically symmetrical? In the human being, there are so
many forces being born which do not, at their beginnings, know
the monotonous fatality of death! One dies only once. But psy-

---

[15] Jean Follain, *Chef-lieu*, p. 201.

chologically we are born many times. Childhood flows from so many springs (*sources*) that it would be as futile to try to construct its geography as to write its history. Thus the poet says:

> Of childhoods I have so many
> That I would get lost counting them.[16]

All these psychic glimmers from roughed-out births (*naissances ébauchées*) shed light on a cosmos being born, the cosmos of limbo. Glimmers and limbo, there then is the dialectic of the antecedence of the being of childhood. A word dreamer cannot help being sensitive to the softness of speech which puts glimmers (*lueurs*) and limbo (*limbes*) under the influence of two labiates. With the glimmer there is water in the light, and Limbo is aquatic. And we shall always return to the same oneiric certainty: Childhood is a human water, a water which comes out of the shadows. This childhood in the mists and glimmers, this life in the slowness of limbo gives us a certain layer of births. What a lot of beings we have begun! What a lot of lost springs which have, nevertheless, flowed! Reverie toward our past then, reverie looking for childhood seems to bring back to life lives which have never taken place, lives which have been imagined. Reverie is a mnemonics of the imagination. In reverie we re-enter into contact with possibilities which destiny has not been able to make use of. A great paradox is connected with our reveries toward childhood: in us, this dead past has a future, the future of its living images, the *reverie future* which opens before any rediscovered image.

V

The great dreamers of childhoods are attracted by this beyond of the birth. Karl Philipp Moritz who, in his book *Anton Reiser*, was able to write an autobiography where his dreams (*rêves*) and memories are woven tightly together, haunted these preambles to existence. He says that the ideas of childhood are perhaps the imperceptible bond which attaches us to former states, at least if what is now our I has existed once before under other conditions.

"Our childhood would then be the Lethe where we had drunk

---

16 Alexandre Arnoux, *Petits poèmes*, Paris, Seghers, p. 31.

in order not to dissolve in the former and future All, to have a suitably limited personality. We are placed in a sort of labyrinth; we do not find the thread which would show us the way out and, doubtless, it is essential that we do not find it. That is why we attach the thread of History to the place where the thread of our (personal) memories breaks, and when our own existence escapes us, we live in that of our ancestors." [17]

The child psychologist will be quick to label such reveries "metaphysical." For him they will be entirely futile since they are not common to everyone or since the maddest of dreamers would not dare to speak them. But the fact is there; this reverie has taken place. It has received the dignity of writing from a great dreamer, a great writer. And these madnesses and futile dreams, these aberrant pages find readers whom they captivate. After having quoted Moritz, Albert Béguin adds that Carl Gustav Carus, a doctor and psychologist, said that "for observations of this depth, he would give all the memories with which literature is flooded."

The labyrinth dreams evoked by Moritz's reverie cannot be explained by lived experiences. They are not formed with corridor anxieties.[18] It is not with experiences that the great dreamers of childhood pose the question: Where do we come from? Perhaps there is an exit toward clear consciousness, but where was the entry to the labyrinth? Didn't Nietzsche say: "If we wish to outline an architecture which conforms to the structure of our soul . . . , it would have to be conceived in the image of the Labyrinth." [19] A soft-walled labyrinth through which, wending his way, slips the dreamer. And from one dream to the other, the labyrinth changes.

A "night of time" is within us. The one which we "learn" through prehistory, through history, through the line of "dynas-

---

17 Quoted by Albert Béguin, *L'âme romantique et le rêve*, 1st edition, vol. I, pp. 83–84. Saint John Perse's stanzas must be read in this penumbral consciousness: ". . . Who still knows the place of his birth?" (quoted by Alain Bosquet, *Saint John Perse*, ed. Seghers, p. 56).
18 In analyzing such reveries, neither do we have to bring up the traumatism of birth studied by the psychoanalyst, Otto Rank. Such nightmares, such sufferings are in the domain of the *nocturnal dream*. Later we shall have the opportunity to underline once again the profound difference which separates the oneirism of night dreams from the oneirism of waking reverie.
19 Nietzsche, *Aurore*, translated, p. 169.

ties" could never be an experienced "night of time." What dreamer will ever be able to understand how one makes a millenium out of ten centuries? May we be left then to dream without numbers about our youth, about our childhood, about Childhood. Ah! how faraway are those times! How ancient is our intimate millenium! the one which is ours, within us, very close to engulfing the before-us? When one dreams in depth, he is never finished beginning. Novalis has written: "Aller wirklicher Anfang ist ein zweiter Moment." (Every effective beginning is a second moment.)[20]

In such a reverie toward childhood, the depth of time is not a metaphor borrowed from spatial measurement. The depth of time is concrete, concretely temporal. Dreaming with a great dreamer of childhood like Moritz is sufficient to make one tremble before this depth.

When, at the pinnacle of age, at the end of age, one sees such reveries, he draws back a bit, for he recognizes that *childhood is the well of being.* Dreaming this way about unfathomable childhood which is one archetype, I am well aware that I am taken by another archetype. The well is an archetype, one of the gravest images of the human soul.[21]

That black and distant water can mark a childhood. It has reflected an astonished face. Its mirror is not that of the fountain. A narcissus can take no pleasure there. Already in his image living beneath the earth, the child does not recognize himself. A mist is on the water; plants which are too green frame the mirror. A cold blast breathes in the depths. The face which comes back in this night of the earth is a face from another world. Now, if a memory of such reflections comes into a memory, isn't it the memory of a before-world?

A well marked my early childhood. I only approached it with my hand tightly clasped in my grandfather's hand. Who was afraid then, the grandfather or the child? And yet the curb was

---

20 Novalis Schriften, ed. Minor, Iena, 1907, vol. II, p. 179.
21 Juan Ramón Jiménez (*Platero et moi*, translated ed. Seghers, p. 64), writes: "The well! . . . What a profound, glaucous, fresh, sonorous word! Wouldn't one say that it is the word itself which bores, while turning, the obscure earth until it reaches fresh water." A word dreamer cannot pass by such a reverie without noting it.

high. It was in a garden which was soon to be lost . . . But a dull evil has remained with me. I know what a well of being is. And since one must tell everything when he is evoking his childhood, I must admit that the well of my greatest terrors was always the well of my goose game. In the middle of the softest evenings, I was more afraid of it than of the skull and crossed tibias.[22]

VI

What a tension of childhoods there must be, held in reserve at the bottom of our being, for a poet's image to make us suddenly relive our memories, reimagining our images by starting from well assembled words. For the poet's image is a spoken image; it is not an image which our eyes see. One feature of the spoken image is sufficient for us to read the poem as the echo of a vanished past.

In order to restore, it is necessary to beautify. The poet's image gives our memories a halo once again. We are far from having an exact memory (*mémoire*) which could keep the memory (*souvenir*) pure by framing it. For Bergson, it seems that pure memories are framed images. Why would one remember having learned a lesson on a garden bench? As if his goal were to fix a point in history! It would at least be necessary, since he is in a garden, to retell the reveries which distracted our schoolboy attention. The pure memory can only be recovered in reverie. It does not come at a given moment to help us in active life. Bergson is an intellectual who does not know himself. By a fatality of his own time, he believes in the *psychic fact,* and his doctrine of memory remains, all things considered, a doctrine of the utility of memory. Com-

---

[22] In Karl Philipp Moritz's novel, *Andreas Hartknopf,* one reads a passage which, for us, makes the well live again in all its archetypal characteristics. "When Andreas was a child he had asked his mother where he had come from. And his mother answered him by showing him the well near their house. In his solitudes, the child returned to the well. His reveries in front of the well would sound the origins of his being. The child's mother would come and tear him away from this obsession with the origin, this obsession with the water lost in the depths of the earth. The well is too strong an image for a dreaming child." And Moritz, in a note which ought to strike a word dreamer, adds that the word "well" was enough to bring back to Hartknopf's soul the memory of the most distant childhood (cf. Karl Philipp Moritz, *Andreas Hartknopf,* (Berlin, 1786) pp. 54-55).

pletely involved in developing a practical psychology, Bergson did not encounter the fusion of memory and reverie.

And yet, how often the pure memory, the useless memory of the useless childhood, comes back to nourish reverie as a benefit of the non-life which helps us live an instant on the edge of life. In a dialectical philosophy of repose and act, of reverie and thought, the memory of childhood tells clearly enough the utility of the useless! It gives us an ineffectual past in real life but one which is suddenly dynamized in that life, imagined or reimagined, which is beneficial reverie. In the growing-old age, the memory of childhood returns us to the delicate sentiments, to that "smiling regret" of the great Baudelairean atmospheres. In the "smiling regret" which the poet experiences, we seem to realize the strange synthesis of regret and consolation. A beautiful poem makes us pardon a very ancient grief.

To live in this atmosphere of another time, we must desocialize our memory and, beyond memories told, retold and recounted by ourselves and by others, by all those who have taught us how we were in the first childhood, we must find our unknown being, the sum total of all the unknowable elements that make up the soul of a child. When reverie goes so far, one is astonished by his own past, astonished to have been that child. There are moments in childhood when every child is the astonishing being, the being who realizes the *astonishment of being*. We thus discover within ourselves an *immobile childhood*, a *childhood without becoming*, liberated from the gearwheels of the calendar.

Then, the time of men no longer reigns over memory any more than the time of saints, those journeymen of everyday time who mark the life of the child only by the first names of his relations; but it is the time of the four divinities of the sky, the seasons. The pure memory has no date. It has a *season*. The season is the fundamental mark of memories. What sun or what wind was there that memorable day? That is the question which gives the right tension of reminiscence. Then the memories become great images, magnified, magnifying images. They are associated with the universe of a season, a season which does not deceive and which can well be called the *total season*, reposing in the immobility of perfection. Total season because all its images speak the same values, because you possess its essence with one particular image such as that dawn which arose out of the memory of a poet:

> What dawn, torn silk
> In the blue of the heat
> Has arisen remembered?
> What movements of colors? [23]

Winter, autumn, sun, the summer river are all roots of total seasons. They are not only spectacles through sight, they are soul values, direct, immobile, indestructible psychological values. Experienced in the memory, they are *always beneficial.* They are lasting benefits. For me summer remains the bouquet season. Summer is a bouquet, an eternal bouquet which could not wilt. For it always takes on the youth of its symbol; it is an offering, very new, very fresh.

The seasons of memory are beautifying. When one goes off dreaming to the bottom of their simplicity, into the very center of their value, the seasons of childhood are the seasons of the poet.

These seasons find the means to be singular while remaining universal. They circle in the sky of Childhood and mark each childhood with indelible signs. Thus our great memories lodge within the zodiac of memory, of a cosmic memory which does not need the precisions of the social memory in order to be psychologically faithful. It is the very memory of our belonging to the world, to a world commanded by the dominating sun. With each season there resounds in us one of the dynamisms of our entry into the world, that entry into the world which so many philosophers bring up at any time and for any reason. The season opens the world, worlds where each dreamer sees his being blossom. And the seasons, armed with their original dynamism, are the seasons of Childhood. Later, the seasons can make a mistake, develop badly, overlap, or fade. But during our childhood, they never make a mistake with signs. Childhood sees the World illustrated, the World with its original colors, its true colors. The great *once-upon-a-time (autrefois)* which we relive by dreaming in our memories of childhood is precisely the world of the *first time.*

---

[23] Noël Ruet, "Le bouquet de sang," *Cahiers de Rochefort,* p. 50.

All the summers of our childhood bear witness to "the eternal summer." The seasons of memory are eternal because they are faithful to the colors of the *first time*. The cycle of exact seasons is a major cycle of the imagined universes. It marks the life of our illustrated universes. In our reveries we see our illustrated universe once more with its *childhood colors*.

VII

Every childhood is prodigious, naturally prodigious. It is not that it lets itself be impregnated, as we are tempted to believe, by the ever so artificial fables which are told to it and which serve only to amuse the ancestor doing the telling. What a lot of grandmothers take their grandson for a little fool! But the child being born malicious stirs up the mania for storytelling, the eternal repetitions of romancing old age. The child's imagination does not live from these fossile fables, these fossiles of fables. It is in his own fables. The child finds his fables in his reverie, fables which he tells no one. Then the fable is life itself: "I have lived without knowing that I was living my fable." This great line is found in a poem entitled "I am sure of nothing." [24] The *permanent child* alone can return the fabulous world to us. Edmond Vandercammen appeals to childhood to "sweep closer to the sky:" [25]

> The sky is waiting to be touched by a hand
>   Of fabulous childhood
> —Childhood, my desire, my queen, my cradlesong—
>   By a breath of the morning.

Besides, how could we tell our *fables* when, precisely, we speak of them as "fables"? We hardly know what a *sincere fable* is any more. Grown-ups write children's stories too easily. Thus they make childish fables. To enter into the fabulous times, it is necessary to be serious like a dreaming child. The fable does not amuse; it enchants. We have lost the language of enchantment. Thoreau wrote: "It seems that we only languish during maturity in order to tell the dreams of our childhood, and they vanish

---

[24] Jean Rousselot, *Il n'y pas d'exil.* Paris, Seghers, p. 41.
[25] Edmond Vandercammen, *Faucher plus près du ciel,* p. 42.

from our memory before we were able to learn their language." [26]
In order to rediscover the language of fables, it is necessary to participate in the existentialism of the fabulous, to become body and soul an admiring being and replace perception of the world with admiration. Admiration in order to receive the qualities of what is perceived. And even in the past, to admire the memory. When Lamartine returned to Saint-Point in 1849, at a site where he was about to relive the past, he wrote: "My soul was nothing but a canticle of illusions." [27] Confronted with witnesses to the past, with objects and sites which recall memories and make them precise, the poet discovers the union of the poetry of memory and the truth of illusions. Childhood memories relived in reverie are really "canticles of illusions" at the bottom of the soul.

VIII

The further one goes toward the past, the more indissoluble the psychological memory-imagination mixture appears. To participate in the existentialism of the poetic, one must reinforce the union of imagination and memory. To do that, it is necessary to rid oneself of the historian's memory which imposes its ideative prerogatives. It is no living memory which runs along the scale of dates without staying long enough at the sites of memory. Memory-imagination makes us live non-event situations in an existentialism of the poetic which gets rid of accidents. To go even further, we live a poetic essentialism. In our reverie which imagines while remembering, our past takes on substance again. Over and above the picturesque, the bonds between the world and the human soul are strong. Then there lives within us not a memory of history but a memory of the cosmos. *Times when nothing happened* come back. Great, beautiful times from the former life when the dreaming being dominated all boredom. A good writer from my native Champagne wrote: ". . . boredom is the greatest provincial happiness. I mean that deep, irremediable boredom which, by its violence, breaks reverie loose within us . . ." [28] Such

---

[26] Henry David Thoreau, *Walden*. Translated by R. Michaud and S. David, p. 48.
[27] Lamartine, *Les foyers du peuple*, 1st series, p. 172.
[28] Louis Ulbach, *Voyage autour de mon clocher*, p. 199.

times manifest their permanence in a rediscovered imagination. They are included in a different duration from experienced duration, in that non-duration which provides the great reposes experienced in an existentialism of the poetic. In those times when nothing was happening, the world was so beautiful! We were in the universe of calm, the universe of reverie. Those great times of non-life dominate life, deepen the past of a person by detaching it, through solitude, from contingencies foreign to his being. Living in a life which dominates life, in a duration which does not endure, has a prestige which the poet knows how to restore within us. Christiane Burucoa writes: "You were, you lived and you did not endure." [29] Poets more than biographers give us the essence of these cosmos memories. Baudelaire touches squarely on this sensitive point: "True memory, considered from the philosophical point of view, consists, I think, only in an imagination which is very lively, easily moved and consequently susceptible to evoking, with the help of each sensation, scenes from the past by giving them something like the enchantment of life." [30]

Here, it seems, Baudelaire is not yet alluding to anything but the photographing of a memory, a sort of instinct which makes a great soul compose the image which is going to be confided to memory. It is reverie which provides the time to accomplish this aesthetic composition. It surrounds the real with enough light for the picture taking to be ample. In the same way, brilliant photographers know how to give duration to their snapshots, very exactly a *duration of reverie*. The poet does the same thing. Then what we confide to our memory, in accord with the existentialism of the poetic is *ours*, belongs to us, is us. It is necessary to possess the center of the image with our whole soul. Too minutely noted circumstances would prejudice the profound being of the memory. They are paraphrases which disturb the great silent memory.

The major problem with the existentialism of the poetic is the maintenance of the state of reverie. We ask great writers to transmit their reveries to us, confirm us in our reveries and thus permit us to live in our reimagined past.

---

[29] Christiane Burucoa, "L'ombre et la proie," *Les cahiers de Rochefort*, no. 3, p. 14.
[30] Baudelaire, *Curiosités esthétiques*, p. 160.

So many passages by Henri Bosco come to aid us in reimagining our own past! In his notes on the Convalescence—isn't every convalescence a childhood?—we shall find a whole ordered pre-ontology of the being which begins to be again by grouping happy and salutary images. Let us reread the admirable page 156 of the tale *Hyacinthe:* "I was not losing consciousness, but at times I was taking nourishment from the original offerings of life, of some sensations which had come from the world; and at other times I would nourish myself from an interior substance. A rare and parsimonious substance, but one which owed nothing to new additions. For if everything was abolished in my real memory, everything on the other hand was living with extraordinary freshness in an imaginary memory. In the middle of vast expanses made barren by forgetfulness, there glowed continuously that marvelous childhood which it seemed to me that I had once invented . . .

"For it was my youth, mine, the one which I had created for myself, and not that youth which a sadly followed childhood had imposed upon me from without." [31]

Listening to Bosco we hear the voice of our reverie which calls us to reimagine our past. We go into a very nearby elsewhere where reality and reverie are indistinguishable. That is where the *Other-House* is, the House of an *Other-Childhood,* constructed with all that *should-have-been* upon a being which was not and which suddenly takes a notion to be and constitutes itself as the home of our reverie.

When I read passages like those by Bosco, I become jealous; how much better he dreams than I, I who dream so much! At least by following him I proceed to impossible syntheses of the places of dispersed dreams in the happy homes along the course of my years. The reverie toward childhood allows us a condensation, in one single place, of the ubiquity of the dearest memories. This condensation adds the house of the beloved to the house of the father, as if all those whom we have loved were, at the summit of our age, supposed to live together, remain together. The biographer, history in hand, would tell us that we are mistaken; our

---

[31] Henri Bosco, *Hyacinthe,* p. 157.

beloved was not in our life in the great days of the grape harvest. Our father was not there in the evenings before the grate when the tea kettle was singing. . .

But why would my reverie know my history? Reverie extends history precisely to the limits of the unreal. It is true in spite of all the anachronisms. It is many times true in its facts and in its values. In reverie, image values become psychological facts. And into the life of a reader there come reveries which the writer has made so beautiful that the writer's reveries become reveries experienced for the reader. By reading "childhoods," my childhood is enriched. The writer has already received the benefit of a "written reverie" which surpasses, by its function, what the writer has experienced. Henri Bosco says further: "Beside the heavy past of my true existence, subjected to the fates of matter, in a full-blown breath, I had a past in harmony with my interior destinies. And by coming back to life, I would go quite naturally to the naive delights of this unreal memory." [32]

When the convalescence is over, when the unreal childhood is going to be lost in an uncertain past, the dreamer in Bosco can say, upon finding a few real memories: "My memories do not recognize me . . . it was I and not they who appeared immaterial." [33]

The passages which are so airy and profound at the same time are composed of images which could be memories. In reveries toward the past, the writer knows how to put a kind of hope into melancholy, an imaginary youth into a memory (*mémoire*) which does not forget. We are really dealing with a psychology of frontiers as if true memories hesitated a little to cross over a frontier in order to win their liberty.

How often in his work Henri Bosco has frequented this frontier, has lived between history and legend, between memory and imagination! In that strangest of his books, in *Hyacinthe* where he performs a great operation in the existentialism of imagined psychology, doesn't he say: "From an imaginary memory, I retained a whole childhood which I did not yet know to be mine

---

[32] Henri Bosco, *loc. cit.*, p. 157.
[33] Henri Bosco, *loc. cit.*, p. 168.

and yet which I did recognize." [34] The reverie which the writer leads in real life has all the oscillations of childhood reveries between the real and the unreal, between real life and imaginary life. Bosco writes: "It was no doubt the forbidden childhood of which I would dream when I was a child. I was rediscovering myself, strangely sensitive, passionate . . . I was living in a calm, familiar house which I had not owned, with playmates, as I had sometimes dreamed of having." [35]

Ah! does the child who exists within us remain under the sign of the forbidden childhood? We are now in the realm of images, of images which are freer than memories. The prohibition to be lifted in order to dream freely does not depend upon psychoanalysis. Beyond parental complexes, there are anthropocosmic complexes against which reverie helps us to react. These complexes block the child in what we shall call, as Bosco does, the forbidden childhood. All our child dreams have to be taken up again so that they will take on their full poetic flight. This task should be accomplished by poetico-analysis. But in order to try it out, it would be necessary to be both poet and psychologist. That is a great deal to ask of one man. And when I see the past again, I can only recall, with each image, these lines which in turn console and torment me, these lines by a poet who also wonders what an image is:

> And often it is nothing but a bubble of childhood
> Under the lentisci of grief.[36]

IX

In our dreams (*songes*) toward childhood, in the poems we would all want to write in order to make our original reveries live again, to give us back the universe of happiness, childhood appears, in the very style of the psychology of the depths, like a real *archetype*, the archetype of simple happiness. It is surely an image within us, a center for images which attract happy images and

[34] *Loc. cit.*, p. 84.
[35] *Loc. cit.*, p. 85.
[36] Jean Rousselot, *Il n'y pas d'exil*. Paris, Seghers, p. 10.

repulse the experiences of unhappiness. But this image, in its principle, is not completely ours; it has deeper roots than our simple memories. Our childhood bears witness to the childhood of man, of the being touched by the glory of living.

From then on, personal memories, clear and often retold, will never completely explain why reveries which carry us back toward our childhood have such an attraction, such a soul quality. The reason for this quality which resists the experiences of life is that childhood remains within us a principle of deep life, of life always in harmony with the possibilities of new beginnings. Everything that begins in us with the distinctness of a beginning is a madness of life. The great archetype of life beginning brings to every beginning the psychic energy which Jung has recognized in every archetype.

Like the archetypes of fire, water and light, childhood, which is a water, a fire which becomes a light, causes a great abundance of fundamental archetypes. In our reveries toward childhood, all the archetypes which link man to the world, which provide a poetic harmony between man and the universe, are, in some sort, revitalized.

We ask our reader not to reject this notion of the *poetic harmony* of archetypes without close scrutiny. We should so much like to be able to demonstrate that poetry is a synthesizing force for human existence! From our point of view, the archetypes are reserves of enthusiasm which help us believe in the world, love the world, create our world. What a lot of concrete life would be given to the philosopheme of the opening on the world if the philosophers were to read the poets! Each archetype is an opening on the world, an invitation to the world. From each opening bursts forth a reverie of flight. And the reverie toward childhood returns us to the virtues of the original reveries. The water of the child, the child's fire, the child's trees, the child's springtime flowers . . . what a lot of true principles for an analysis of the world!

If the word "analysis" must have a meaning when one is touching a childhood, it is then necessary to say that one analyzes a childhood better with poems than with memories, better with reveries than with facts. It is meaningful, we believe, to speak of a poetic analysis of man. The psychologists do not know everything. Poets have other insights into man.

To meditate on the child we were, beyond all family history, after going beyond the zone of regrets, after dispersing all the mirages of nostalgia, we reach an anonymous childhood, a pure threshold of life, original life, original human life. And this life is within us—let us underline that once again—remains within us. A dream (*songe*) brings us back to it. The memory does nothing more than open the door to the dream (*songe*). The archetype is there, immutable, immobile beneath memory, immobile beneath the dreams (*songes*). And when one has made the archetypal power of childhood come back to life through dreams, all the great archetypes of the paternal forces, maternal forces take on their action again. The father is there, also immobile. The mother is there, also immobile. Both escape time. Both live with us in another time. And everything changes; the fire of long ago is different from today's fire. Everything which welcomes has the virtue of an origin. And the archetypes will always remain origins of powerful images.

An analysis through archetypes taken as sources of poetic images benefits from a great homogeneity; for archetypes often join forces. Under their reign, the childhood is without complexes. In his reveries the child realizes the unity of poetry.

Correlatively, if one does a psychoanalysis with the aid of poems, if one takes a poem as a tool of analysis to measure its resonance at different depth levels, he will sometimes succeed in reviving abolished reveries, forgotten memories. With an image which is not ours, sometimes with a very singular image, we are called to dream in depth. The poet has touched the right chord. His emotion moves us; his enthusiasm buoys us. And in the same way, "recounted fathers" have nothing in common with our father—nothing in common, if not, in the great accounts of the poets, the *depth of an archetype*. Then reading is covered with dreams and becomes a dialogue with our dead relations.

Dreamed and meditated, meditated in the very intimacy of solitary reverie, childhood takes on the tonality of a philosophical poem. A philosopher who makes a place for dreams (*songes*) in "philosophical reflection" comes to know, with the meditated childhood, a *cogito* which emerges from the shadows, which retains a fringe of shadow which is perhaps the *cogito* of a "shadow." This *cogito* is not immediately transformed into certainty like the professors' *cogito*. Its light is a glimmer which does not know its origin. There, existence is never quite assured. Besides, why exist since you are dreaming? Where does life begin? In the life which does not dream or in the life which does dream? When was the first time, wonders the dreamer? In memory everything is clear—but in the reverie which is attached to the memory? It seems that this reverie bounces back from unfathomable depths. The childhood is constituted of fragments in the time of an indefinite past, a messy sheaf of vague beginnings. The *immediately* is a temporal function of clear thought, of the life which unfolds on one single level. In meditating on the reverie in order to descend to the securities of the archetype, it is necessary, shall we say, "to deepen" (*profonder*) it, to use an expression which certain alchemists liked to use.

Thus, taken in the perspective of its archetypal qualities, put back into the cosmos of great archetypes which are at the base of the human soul, meditated childhood is more than the sum of our memories. To understand our attachment to the world, it is necessary to add a childhood, our childhood to each archetype. We cannot love water, fire, the tree without putting a love into them, a friendship which goes back to our childhood. We love them with childhood. When we love all these beauties of the world now in the song of the poets, we love them in a new found childhood, in a childhood reanimated with that childhood which is latent in each of us.

Thus, the word from a poet, the new but archetypally true image is enough to make us recover the universes of childhood. Without childhood, there is no real cosmicity. Without cosmic song, there is no poetry. The poet awakens within us the cosmicity of childhood.

Later we shall be giving many images where the poets cause, in Minkowski's sense of the word, a "resonance" of the archetypes of childhood and cosmicity within us.

For that is the decisive phenomenological fact; childhood, in its archetypal quality, is *communicable*. A soul is never deaf to a *quality of childhood*. However singular the feature being evoked, if it has the sign of childhood primitiveness, it awakens within us the archetype of childhood. Childhood, a sum of the insignificances of the human being, has a proper phenomenological meaning, a pure phenomenological meaning since it is under the sign of wonder. By the poet's grace we have become the pure and simple subject of the verb "to marvel."

What a lot of proper nouns come to wound, rag and break the anonymous child of solitude! And in memory itself, too many faces come back to prevent us from finding the memories of times when we were alone, very much alone in the profound boredom of being alone, free too to think of the world, free to see the sun setting, the smoke rising from a roof, all those great phenomena which one sees badly when he is not looking at them alone.

Smoke rising from a roof! . . . a hyphen uniting the village with the sky . . . In memories it is always blue, slow, light. Why?

When we are children, people *show* us so many things that we lose the profound sense of *seeing*. Seeing and showing are phenomenologically in violent antithesis. And just how could adults show us the world they have lost!

They know; they think they know; they say they know. . . . They demonstrate to the child that the earth is round, that it revolves around the sun. And the poor dreaming child has to listen to all that! What a release for your reverie when you leave the classroom to go back up the side hill, your side hill!

What a cosmic being the dreaming child is!

X

Between the light melancholy from which all reverie is born and the distant melancholy of a child who has dreamed a lot, there is profound harmony. Through the melancholy of the dreaming (*songeur*) child, the melancholy of all reverie has a past. A continuity of being, the continuity of the existentialism of the dreaming being is formed in this harmony. No doubt, we are familiar with reveries which prepare our vigor, give dynamism to our projects. But they tend precisely to break with the past. They nourish a revolt. Now, the revolts which remain in childhood memories do not feed today's intelligent revolts very well. It is the psychoanalysts' function to cure them. But melancholy reveries are not noxious. They even help our repose; they give body to our repose.

If our research on natural reverie, on restful reverie could be pursued, it should constitute itself in a complementary doctrine of psychoanalysis. Psychoanalysis studies the *life of events*. We are trying to know life without events, a life which does not mesh with the lives of others. It is the lives of the others which bring events into our life. In comparison with this life attached to its peace, this life without events, all events risk being "traumas," masculine brutalities which trouble the natural peace of our *anima*, the feminine being within us which, let us repeat, lives well only in its reverie.

Softening, erasing the traumatic character of certain childhood memories, the salutary task of psychoanalysis, returns to dissolve those psychic concretions formed around a singular event. But a substance does not dissolve in nothingness. In order to dissolve the unfortunate concretions, reverie offers us its calm waters, the obscure waters which sleep at the bottom of every life. Water, water always comes to calm us. In any event, the restful reveries must find a substance of repose.

If night and its nightmares are the domain of psychoanalysis, the reverie of the beautiful times of repose only needs to be maintained by a consciousness of tranquility in order to be positively salutary. It is the very function of a phenomenology of reverie to redouble the benefit of reverie through a consciousness of reverie. The poetics of reverie no longer has to determine anything but the interests of a reverie which maintain the dreamer in a consciousness of tranquility.

Here, in a reverie toward childhood, the poet calls us to conscious tranquility. He offers to transmit to us the tranquilizing power of reverie. But, to repeat, this tranquility has substance, the substance of a tranquil melancholy. Without the substance of melancholy, this tranquility would be empty. It would be the tranquility of nothing.

One can then understand that what draws us toward the reveries of childhood is a sort of nostalgia of nostalgia. The poet of pale, immobile waters, Georges Rodenbach, knows this redoubled nostalgia. It seems that what he regrets from childhood is not the joys but the tranquil sadness, the sadness without cause of the solitary child. Life disturbs us only too often from this radical melancholy. Rodenbach owes the unity of his poetic genius to this childhood melancholy. There are readers who may think that meloncholy poetry is monotonous. But if our reverie makes us sensitive to forgotten nuances, Rodenbach's poems teach us to dream gently again, to dream faithfully. Reveries toward childhood: the nostalgia of faithfulness!

Thus poem XIV in *The Mirror of the Native Sky* (1898), in each of its stanzas, revives the original melancholy:

> Gentleness of the past which one remembers
> Across the mists of time
> And the mists of the memory.
>
> Gentleness of seeing oneself as a child again,
> In the old house of stones too black
>
> .   .   .   .
> Gentleness of recovering one's thinner face
> As a pensive child, forehead against the windowpane. . . .

Flamboyant poetry, poetry with ringing syllables, looking for the burst of sounds and colors, will have very little sympathy for this pensive child, "forehead against the windowpane." People do not read Rodenbach anymore. But a childhood is there: idle childhood, childhood which, by getting bored, knows the *harmonious* cloth of life. In reverie tinged with melancholy, the dreamer knows the existentialism of the tranquil life within this cloth. Then with the poet we return to the beaches of childhood, far from every tempest.

In the same poem, Rodenbach writes (page 63):

> Has one been that child there before him?
> Silent and sad childhood
> Which never laughs.

and on page 64:

> Child too nostalgic and feeling sad
> . . . .
> Child who never played, child too good
> Child whose soul was too caught up in the North
> Ah! that noble, that pure child one was
> And whom one remembers
> All his life . . .

Thus, very simply, the poet puts us in the presence of a *state-of-being memory* (*souvenir d'état*). In a poem without color, without events, we recognize *states* which we have known; for in the most turbulent, the most joyous childhood, aren't there times "in the North?"

These times without a clock are still within us. Propitious and appeasing, reverie gives them back to us. They are simply but nobly human. All the words of Rodenbach's poem are true and if we dream upon such a poem, we soon recognize that these words are not superficial; they call us to the depths of memories. Within us, among all our childhoods, there is the melancholy childhood, a childhood which already possessed human nobility and seriousness. The memory tellers hardly ever tell about it. How could they induce us to sojourn in a state when they are recounting events? Perhaps we need a poet to reveal such *qualities of being*. In any case, reverie toward childhood will experience a great benefit of repose if it deepens itself by following the reverie of a poet.

Within us, still within us, always within us, childhood is a state of mind.

XI

We find this state of mind in our reveries; it comes to help us put our being to rest. It is really childhood without its turbulence. One can, of course, have the memory of being a difficult child. But the acts of anger of this distant past do not revitalize today's anger. Psychologically, the hostile events are now disarmed. True reverie could not be ill-tempered; reverie toward childhood, the most subdued of our reveries, must bring us peace.

In a recent thesis, André Saulnier has studied "the spirit of child-hood" in Mme Guyon's work.[37] It goes without saying that for a religious soul, childhood can appear as innocence incarnate. The adoration of the Divine Child makes that soul live which prays in an atmosphere of original innocence. But the expression "origi-nal innocence" makes too easy a conquest of its significance. Finer moral research is necessary to stabilize psychological values. Such moral research ought to help us reconstitute within us the spirit of childhood and above all to apply the spirit of childhood in our complex lives. In this "application," the childhood which subsists within us must truly become the *subject* of our life of love, the subject of our acts of oblation, our good acts. Through "the spirit of childhood," Mme Guyon recovers simple, natural goodness without argument. The benefit is so great that, for Mme Guyon, grace must intervene, a grace which comes from Christ Child. Mme Guyon writes: "I was, as I have said, in a state of childhood: when I had to speak or write, there was nothing greater than I; it seemed to me that I was all full of God; and yet, that there was nothing smaller, weaker than I; for I was as a little child. Our Lord not only wanted me to bear His state of Childhood in a way which would charm those who could be charmed, but He also wanted me to begin honoring His divine Childhood with an ex-terior cult. He inspired that good mendicant friar of whom I have spoken to send me a Christ Child in wax, and one of ravishing beauty; and I noticed that the more I looked at it the more the dispositions of childhood were impressed upon me. One cannot imagine the difficulty I had in abandoning myself to this state of childhood; for my reason lost itself in it, and it seemed to me that it was I who was giving this state to me. When I had been reflect-ing, it would be taken from me and I would enter into intoler-able pain; but as soon as I abandoned myself, I would find inside myself a candor, an innocence, a child's simplicity and something divine." [38]

Kierkegaard understood how metaphysically great man would be if the child were his master. In the meditation entitled "The

[37] André Saulnier, *L'esprit d'enfance dans la vie et la poésie de Mme Guyon,* unpublished thesis.
[38] Madame Guyon, *Oeuvres,* vol. II p. 267 (quoted by Saulnier, *loc. cit.,* p. 74).

Lilies of the Fields and the Birds of the Skies," he writes: "And who would teach me the good heart of a child! When the imaginary or real need plunges one into worry and discouragement, makes one surly or disheartened, one likes to feel the beneficial influence of a child, to learn from him and, once one's soul is calmed, call him one's master with gratitude." [39] We need lessons so badly from a life which is beginning, from a soul which is blossoming, from a mind that is opening! In the great misfortunes of life, one takes courage when he is the guardian of a child. In his meditation, Kierkegaard is taking aim at the destiny of eternity. But the images of his beautiful book act on a humble life which does not have the certainties of faith. And in order to enter into the very spirit of Kierkegaard's meditation, it must be said that worry sustains. Worry about the child sustains an invincible courage. Mme Guyon's "spirit of childhood" receives an afflux of will from Kierkegaard.

XII

The scope of the present essay does not permit us to follow the research of mythologists who have shown the importance of myths of childhood in the history of religions. By studying the work of Karl Kerenyi among others, it will be evident what a perspective for the deepening of the being can take form in a sanctified childhood.[40] For Kerenyi, the child in Mythology is a clear example of the *mythologeme*. In order to grasp fully the value and action of this mythologeme, of this accession of a being into mythology, the course of a biography must be stopped; the child must be given such relief that his state of childhood can reign permanently over life and be an immortal god of life. In a fine article in *Critique* (May, 1959), Hervé Rousseau, studying Kerenyi's work, clearly underlines the isolation of the divine child. This isolation can be due to a human crime: the child is abandoned, his cradle abandoned to the waves and carried far from men. But this preliminary drama is barely experienced in the legends. It is only indi-

---

39 S. Kierkegaard, *Les lis des champs et les oiseaux du ciel*, translated by J.-H. Tisseau, Alcan, 1935, p. 97.
40 Cf. in particular Kerenyi's book written in collaboration with C. G. Jung, *Introduction à l'essence de la Mythologie*, translated by Payot.

cated to underline the detachment of the prestigious child who must not follow a human destiny. The mythologeme of the child expresses, according to Kerenyi, and in Hervé Rousseau's words, "the solitary state of the essentially orphan child but who, in spite of everything, is at home in the original world and loved by the gods."(*Loc. cit.*, p. 439).

An orphan in the family of man and beloved in the family of the gods—those are the two poles of the mythologeme. We must have a great tension of reverie to relive its whole oneirism on the human scale. Are there not reveries where we were somewhat orphaned and where our hopes were tending toward idealized beings, the very gods of our hopes?

But in dreaming on the family of the gods, we would slip into biographies. The mythologeme of childhood invites us to greater dreams (*songes*). For our own reverie, it is in this adherence to the *original cosmos* that we become sensitive to the mythologeme of sanctified (*divinisées*) childhoods. In all the myths of sanctified childhoods, the world takes care of the child. The child god is son of the world. And in the face of this child who represents a continuous birth, the world is young.

From our simple point of view as a dreamer, all these sanctified childhoods are proof of the activity of an archetype which lives in the depths of the human soul. The archetype of the child and the mythologeme of the sanctified child are correlative. Without the archetype of the child, we would receive the numerous examples of mythology as simple historical facts. As we were indicating earlier, in spite of our readings of the works of mythologists, there could be no question for us of classifying the documents which they offer us. The very fact that these documents are numerous proves that the problem of a childhood of divinity has arisen. That is the sign of a permanence of childhood, of a permanence which is living in reveries. In every dreamer there lives a child, a child whom reverie magnifies and stabilizes. Reverie tears it away from history, sets it outside time, makes it foreign to time. One more reverie and this permanent, magnified child is a god.

In any event, when one maintains a trace of childhood within him, he reads everything which touches on the archetype or mythologeme of childhood with more sympathy. He seems to take part in that restitution of the power of abolished dreams. One must, no doubt, master the objectivity in which archaeologists take pride. But this mastered objectivity does not suppress complex interests. How can one not admire what he is studying when he sees the legends of the ages of life surge up from the depths of the past.

XIII

But we are noting these great states of mind in the religious spirit only to indicate a perspective for research in which the child would appear as an ideal of life. We are not exploring the religious horizon. We wish to remain in contact with psychological documents which we can relive personally, in the modesty of our domestic reveries.

But these domestic reveries which we have placed under the dominant tonality of melancholy know variations which modify their character. It seems that melancholy reverie is only an opening to reverie. But it is such a consoling reverie that a happiness of dreaming (*rêver*) animates us. Here is a new nuance which we find in Franz Hellens' great book, *Secret Documents*. Writing of childhood memories, the poet tells us the vital importance of the obligation to write.[41] In slow writing, childhood memories relax, breathe. The peace of childhood life rewards the writer. Franz Hellens knows that childhood memories are not anecdotes.[42] But nourished by legend, the vegetable force of childhood subsists within us throughout our lives. Therein lies the secret of our profound vegetalism. Franz Hellens writes: "Childhood is not a thing which dies within us and dries up as soon as it has completed its cycle. It is not a memory. It is the most living of treasures, and it continues to enrich us without our knowing it . . . Woe to the man who cannot remember his childhood, recapture

---

41 In exile in Paris, Adam Mickiewicz says: "When I write, I seem to be in Lithuania." To write sincerely is to recover one's youth, one's country.
42 Franz Hellens writes (*loc. cit.*, p. 167): "Human history, like that of nations, is made up as much of legends as of reality, and it would not be exaggerating to affirm that legend is a superior reality. I say legend and not anecdote; the anecdote decomposes; the legend constructs." And every human being bears witness, when he is remembering his childhood, to a legendary childhood. At the bottom of memory, every childhood is legendary.

it within himself, like a body inside his own body, a new blood in the old blood: he is dead as soon as it leaves him." [43]

And Hellens quotes Hölderlin: "Don't chase the man away too quickly from the cabin where his childhood was spent." Isn't this request by Hölderlin addressed to the psychoanalyst, that bailiff who believes it his duty to chase man away from the attic of memories where he would go to cry when he was a child? The native house—lost, destroyed, razed—remains the main building for our reveries toward childhood. The shelters of the past welcome and protect our reveries.

When well sheltered, memories are reborn as rays of being rather than as frozen shapes. Franz Hellens confides to us that: "My memory is fragile; I quickly forget the contour, the feature; only the melody remains within me. I have difficulty retaining the object, but I cannot forget the atmosphere, which is the sonority of things and beings." [44] Franz Hellens remembers as a poet.

And what a feeling too, across all the ages of a life, for the solid vegetalism of childhood! Upon meeting Gorki in Italy, Franz Hellens expresses his impression thus: "I found myself before a man who summarized and clarified singularly, in a single look of his blue eyes, the idea I had of maturity, invaded and somehow renewed by the freshness of a childhood which had not stopped growing within him without his knowing it." [45]

A child who does not stop growing; such is precisely the dynamism which animates the reveries of a poet when he is making us live a childhood, when he is suggesting that we relive our childhood.

By following the poet, it seems that if we deepen our reverie toward childhood, we root the tree of our destiny more deeply. The problem of knowing where the destiny of man has its real roots remains open. But beside the real man, more or less capable of straightening the line of his destiny, in spite of the shock of conflicts, in spite of all the troubles of complexes, there is in each man a *destiny of reverie,* a destiny which runs in front of us through our dreams (*songes*) and takes on body in our reveries.

---

[43] Franz Hellens, *loc. cit.*, p. 146.
[44] Franz Hellens, *loc. cit.*, p. 151.
[45] Franz Hellens, *loc. cit.*, p. 161.

Isn't it also in reverie that man is most faithful to himself? And if our dreams (*songes*) nourish our acts a little, it will always be profitable to meditate on our most ancient dreams (*songes*) in the atmosphere of childhood. Franz Hellens has this revelation: "I feel a great relief. I return from a long trip and I have acquired a certainty: the childhood of man poses the problem of his whole life; it is the task of maturity to find a solution to it. I have traveled thirty years with this enigma, without giving it a thought, and today I know that everything had already been said as I set out. The setbacks, unhappiness and discouragements have passed over me, in any case without marking me or tiring me." [46]

Visual images are so clear; they form pictures which summarize life so naturally that they are privileged with easy evocation in our childhood memories. But whoever would wish to penetrate into the zone of indeterminate childhood, into the childhood without proper names and without a history either, would no doubt be helped by the return of the great vague memories like the memories of odors from the past. Odors! the first evidence of our fusion with the world. These memories of odors from the past are recovered by closing our eyes. Long ago we closed our eyes to savor them fully. We closed our eyes and then, right away, we dreamed a little. By dreaming well, by dreaming simply in a tranquil reverie, we are going to find them again. In the past as in the present, a beloved odor is the center of an intimacy. Some memories are faithful to this intimacy. Poets are going to give us testimony on those odors of childhood, on those odors which impregnate the seasons of childhood.

A great writer, whom death took too soon from French poetry, wrote: "My childhood is a sheaf of odors." [47]

And in another work which recounts an adventure far from his native land, Chadourne puts the whole memory (*mémoire*) of the old days under the sign of odors: "Days of our childhood whose torments themselves seem like felicity to us and whose tenacious scent perfumes our late season." [48] When memory breathes, all odors are good. Great dreamers thus know how to breathe the

---

[46] Franz Hellens, *loc. cit.*, p. 173.
[47] Louis Chadourne, *L'inquiète adolescence*, p. 32.
[48] Louis Chadourne, *Le livre de Chanaan*, p. 42.

past; Milosz, for example, "evokes the obscure charm of days
which have fled": "The foamy and somnolent odor of old lodg-
ings is the same in all countries, and very often, in the course of
my solitary pilgrimages to the holy places of memory and nostalgia, it was enough for me to close my eyes in some old dwelling
to carry me back immediately to the somber house of my Danish
ancestors and thus relive, in the space of an instant, all the joys
and all the sadnesses of a childhood accustomed to the tender
odor which was so full of rain and of the sunset in antique
houses." [49] The rooms of the lost house, the corridors, the cellar
and the attic are retreats for faithful odors, odors which the
dreamer knows belong only to him: "Our childhood perpetuates
a velvet perfume." [50]

What astonishment then when, in reading, a singular odor is
communicated to us, restored to the memory of lost times. A season, a *personal season* is contained in this singular odor. For instance:

> . . . the odor of a poor, damp hood
> Through you Autumn

And Louis Chadourne adds:

> Who then does not remember
> —o fraternity
> of a tree, of a house, or of a childhood [51]

For the damp hood through the autumn gives all that, gives a
world.

A damp hood and all our October childhoods, all our schoolboy courages are reborn in our memory. The odor has remained
in the *word*. Proust needed the dough of the madeleine to remember. But already an unexpected word finds the same power
all by itself. What a lot of memories come back to us when poets
tell us their childhood! Here is Chadourne's spring contained in
the fragrance of a bud: "in the bitter, sticky fragrance of buds." [52]

---

[49] O. W. Milosz, *L'amoureuse initiation*, Paris, Grasset, p. 17.
[50] Yves Cosson, *Une croix de par Dieu*, 1958 (unpaginated).
[51] Louis Chadourne, *Accords*, p. 31.
[52] Louis Chadourne, *Accords*, p. 36.

If everyone just looks a bit, he will find the odor of a spring bud in his memory. For me the fragrance of springtime was in the poplar bud. Ah! young dreamers, crush the sticky poplar bud between your fingers, taste that unctuous, bitter dough and you will have enough memories to last all your life.[53]

So in its first expansion, the odor is a root of the world, a truth of childhood. The odor gives us the universes of childhood in expansion. When poets lead us into this domain of vanished odors, they give us poems of great simplicity. Emiliane Kerhoas, in *Saint-Cadou,* speaks thus:

> Fragrant resin
> of ancient days
>
> . . . .
>
> O Paradise of Childhood.

The resin which flows from the tree contains the odor of the whole orchard of the Paradise of our summers.

In a poem entitled "Childhood," Claude-Anne Bozombres says with the same simplicity:

> The fragrance of paths
> hemmed with mint
> dances in my childhood.[54]

Sometimes a singular conjunction of odors recalls, from the bottom of our memory, an odorous nuance so unique that we don't know whether we are dreaming or remembering, as with this treasure of intimate memory: "The mint threw its breath in our faces while the freshness of the moss escorted us in a minor key." [55] By itself, the odor of mint is a complex of warmth and freshness. Here it is orchestrated by the humid softness of the moss. Such an encounter has been experienced, experienced in the distance of life which belongs to another time. It is not a question of experiencing it today. One must dream a great deal to

---

[53] Alain Bosquet (*Premier testament,* p. 47) writes:
    How many memories? how many memories
    Then a very lonely perfume:
    it explained everything to me.
[54] C.-A. Bozombres, *Tutoyer l'arc-en-ciel,* ed. Cahiers de Rochefort, p. 24.
[55] Jacques de Bourbon-Busset, *Le silence et la joie,* p. 110.

find the exact climate of childhood which balances the fire of the mint and the odor of the stream. In any event, one feels plainly that the writer who presents us with this synthesis is breathing his past. Memory and reverie are in total symbiosis.

In his book *Today's Muses* which is subtitled *Essay in Poetic Physiology*, Jean de Gourmont gives great importance to "odorous images, the subtlest, the most untranslatable of all images." [56] He quotes this line by Marie Dauguet: "The harmony of bitter boxwood and musky carnations."

These unions of two odors belong to the past. The mixture takes place in the memory. Sensations which are present would be slaves to their objects. In the distance of the memory, don't the boxwood and carnation return a very ancient garden to us?

Jean de Gourmont sees an application there of Huysmans' formula for assembled synesthesias. But the poet, by putting two odors into the coffer of a line of poetry,[57] preserves them for an indefinite duration. Henri Bosco says that he breathed "the odor of roses and salt" of a childhood snow. That is the very odor of vivifying cold.[58]

A whole vanished universe is preserved by an odor. Lucie Delarue-Mardrus, the beautiful Norman poetess writes: "The odor of my country was an apple." And this line, so often quoted without reference, is by Lucie Delarue-Mardrus: "And who then was ever cured of his childhood." [59] In a life of voyages reinforced by imaginary voyages, there also sounds this cry from the distance of the ages: "Ah! I shall never be cured of my country."

The farther one is from his native land, the more he suffers from the nostalgia of its odors. In a tale of adventures in the faraway West Indies, one of Chadourne's characters receives a letter from an old serving woman who is taking care of his farm in the Perigord. The letter is "so palpitating with humble tenderness, impregnated with the odor of my granary, my root cellar,

[56] Jean de Gourmont, *Muses d' aujourd'hui*, p. 94.
[57] Would that I had the poetic sacredness necessary to open "the tabernacle of the sonnet," as Valéry had the right to do, at twenty. Cf. Henri Mondo, *Les premiers temps d'une amitié* (André Gide et Valéry), p. 15.
[58] Henri Bosco, *Bargabot*, p. 130.
[59] Quoted by Jean de Gourmont, *loc. cit.*, p. 75.

with all those things which were in my senses and in my heart." [60]

All those odors come back together in the syncretism of the memories of childhood times when the old serving woman was the good nurse. Hay and root cellar, the dry and the damp, wine cellar and attic, everything comes together to give the exiled man the total odor of the house.

Henri Bosco is familiar with these indestructible syntheses: "I was raised in the odor of the earth, the wheat and the new wine. When I think about it, a vivid vapor of joy and youth still comes back to me." [61] Bosco proposes the decisive nuance: a *vapor of joy* rises from the memory. Memories are the incense in reserve in the past. A forgotten author has written: "For odors, like musical sounds, are rare sublimators of the essence of memory." As George du Maurier was very easily ironical with regard to himself, he adds parenthetically: "There is a sentence of prodigious subtlety—I hope it means something." [62] But *meaning* is of little importance when it is a question of giving memories their dream (*rêve*) atmosphere. Attached to its odor memories, a childhood smells good. It is in the night's nightmares and not in free reveries that the soul is tormented by the odors of hell, by the sulphur and pitch which burn in the excremental hell where August Strindberg suffered. The house of one's birth does not smell musty. Memory is faithful to the fragrances of the past. A poem by Léon-Paul Fargue tells of this faithfulness to odors:

> Look. The poem of the ages is playing and ringing . . .
> O garden of yesteryear, perfumed night light . . .[63]

Each childhood is a night light in the bedroom of memories.

Jean Bourdeillette says this prayer:

> Master of odors and of things
> Lord
> Why are they dead before me
> Those unfaithful companions.[64]

---

[60] Louis Chadourne, *Terre de Chanaan*, p. 155.
[61] Henri Bosco, *Antonin*, p. 14.
[62] George du Maurier, *Peter Ibbeston*, p. 18.
[63] Léon-Paul Fargue, *Poèmes*, 1912, p. 76.
[64] Jean Bourdeillette, *Reliques des songes*, (Paris, 1958) Seghers, p. 65.

And as the poet wishes with all his soul to maintain the odors in all faithfulness:

> Your odor will sleep in my heart till the end,
> Wilted armchair of childhood.

When, in reading the poets, one discovers that a whole childhood is evoked by the memory of an isolated fragrance, he understands that odor, in a childhood, in a life, is, if we may put it this way, an *immense detail*. This nothing added to the whole works on the very being of the dreamer. This nothing makes him live the magnifying reverie; we read that poet with total sympathy who gives the germ of this enlargement of childhood in an image. When I read this line by Edmond Vandercammen: "My childhood goes back to that wheaten bread," an odor of warm bread invaded a house of my youth. The custard (*flan*) and round loaf returned to my table. Festive occasions are associated with this domestic bread. The world was in joy for the celebration of the warm bread. Two cocks on a single spit were cooking before the scarlet hearth. "A well-buttered sun was roasting in the blue sky."

In days of happiness, the world is edible. And when the great odors which were preparing feasts return to me in memory, it seems to me, Baudelarian that I was, that "I eat memories." Suddenly, I am taken by the urge to collect all the warm bread to be found in poetry. How they would help me give to memory the great odors of the celebration begun again, of a life which one would take up again, swearing gratitude for the original joys.

Four

The "Cogito" of the Dreamer

> For yourself, be a dream
> Of red wheat and smoke
>
> .   .   .
>
> You will never grow old
>> Jean Rousselot,
>> *Agrégation du temps*

> Life is unbearable for the man
> who does not always have an enthusiasm at hand.
>> Maurice Barrès,
>> *Un homme libre*

I

The night dream (*rêve*) does not belong to us. It is not our possession. With regard to us, it is an abductor, the most disconcerting
of abductors: it abducts our being from us. Nights, nights have no
history. They are not linked one to another. And when a person
has lived a lot, when he has already lived some twenty-thousand
nights, he never knows in which ancient, very ancient night he
started off to dream. The night has no future. There are no doubt
nights which are less dark when our day being still lives enough
to traffic with its memories. The psychoanalyst explores these half-
nights. In these half-nights, our being is still there, dragging
along human dramas, all the weight of badly led lives. But already beneath this spoiled life, an abyss of non-being is open
where certain nocturnal dreams are swallowed up. In such absolute dreams, we are returned to an ante-subjective state. We become elusive to ourselves, for we are giving pieces of ourselves to
no matter whom, to no matter what. The nocturnal dream dis-
perses our being over phantoms of unusual beings who are no
longer even shadows of ourselves. The words "phantoms" and
"shadows" are too strong. They are still too well attached to realities. They prevent us from going as far as the extremity of the
obliteration of being, as far as the obscurity of our being dissolv-
ing into the night. The metaphysical sensitivity of the poet helps
us approach our nocturnal abysses. Paul Valéry says that he believes dreams are formed "by some other sleeper, as if in the night,

they mistook the absent person." [1] To go and be absent from the house of beings who are absent, such is precisely absolute flight, the resignation from all the forces of the being, the dispersion of all the beings of our being. Thus we sink into the absolute dream.

What can be recuperated from such a disaster of the being? Are there still sources of life at the bottom of this non-life? What a lot of dreams must be known, in depth and not superficially, in order to determine the dynamism of the outcroppings! If the dream descends deeply enough into the abysses of the being, how can one believe, as the psychoanalysts do, that it always systematically retains social meanings. In the nocturnal life, there are depths where we bury ourselves, where we have the will to live no longer. In these depths, we brush intimately against nothingness, our nothingness. Are there other nothingnesses than the nothingness of our being? All the obliterations of the night converge toward this nothingness of our being. At the limit, absolute dreams plunge us into the universe of the Nothing.

When this Nothing fills up with Water, we are already coming back to life. Then, saved from the ontological drama, we sleep better. Plunged into the waters of good sleep, we are in a balance of being with a universe at peace. But is being in a balance of being with a universe really being? Hasn't the water of sleep dissolved our being? In any case, we become beings with no history upon entering into the realm of the Night which has no history. When we sleep thus in the waters of profound slumber, we sometimes know eddies, but never currents. We experience passing dreams (*rêves*). They are not life dreams. For every dream which we recount upon returning to the light of day, there are many whose thread we have lost. The psychoanalyst does not work at those depths. He believes he can explain lacunae without paying attention to the fact that those black holes which interrupt the line of recounted dreams are perhaps the mark of the death instinct which is working at the bottom of our shadows. Alone, a poet can bring us an image, sometimes, of that distant place, an echo of the ontological drama of a slumber without memory when our being was perhaps being tempted by the non-being.

---

1 Paul Valéry, *Eupalinos. L'âme et la danse. Dialogue de l'arbre.* Paris, Gallimard, p. 199.

Dreams without a history, dreams which could light up only in a perspective of annihilation are in the Nothing or in the Water. It is then self-evident that in such dreams the dreamer will never find a guarantee of his existence. Such nocturnal dreams, those dreams of extreme night, cannot be experiences in which one can formulate a *cogito*. There the subject loses his being; they are dreams without a subject.

Where is the philosopher who will give us the metaphysics of the night, the metaphysics of the human night? The dialectics of black and white, of no and yes, of disorder and order are not sufficient to frame the nothingness at work at the bottom of our sleep. What a distance is covered from the shores of Nothing, that Nothing that we were to this someone, however wan he may be, who is recovering his being beyond sleep! Ah! how can a Mind risk sleeping?

But won't the Metaphysics of the night remain a sum of peripheral views without ever being able to find the lost *cogito* again, a radical *cogito* which would not be the *cogito* of a shadow?

It is then necessary to envisage nocturnal dreams of lesser sleep in order to discover documents of subjective psychology. When the ontic losses of extreme dreams are measured better, people will be more prudent in the ontological determinations of the nocturnal dream. For example, even when it is a question of dreams which have emerged from the night and which can be unwound on the thread of a story, will someone ever tell us the veritable nature of the *inspiriting character*? Is it really us? Always us? Do we recognize our inspiriting being there, that simple habit of becoming which is attached to our being? Even if we can retell it, recover it in its strange becoming, isn't the dream evidence of the lost being, of a being which is getting lost, of a being which is fleeing our being?

Then a philosopher of the dream (*songe*) wonders: can I really pass from the nocturnal dream to the existence of the dreaming subject, as the lucid philosopher passes from the thought—from any thought—to the existence of the being which is thinking it? [2]

---

[2] Night grammar is not the same as the grammar of the day. In the night dream, the function of the *whatever* does not exist. There is no ordinary

In other words, to follow the habits of philosophical language, it does not seem to us that one can speak of a valid *cogito* for a dreamer of nocturnal dreams. It is certainly difficult to trace the frontier which separates the domain of the nocturnal Psyche from that of the daytime Psyche, but this frontier exists. There are two centers of being within us, but the nocturnal center is a blurred center of concentration. It is not a "subject."

Does psychoanalytic inquiry descend all the way to the ante-subject? If it penetrated into that sphere, could it find explanatory elements there for the elucidation of the dramas of the personality? That is a problem which, as far as we are concerned, remains unresolved. It seems to us that human misfortunes do not descend that deeply; man's misfortunes remain "superficial." Deep nights return us to the equilibrium of the stable life.

When one meditates upon the lessons of psychoanalysis, he is already well aware that he is being sent back to the superficial zone, to the socialized zone. Furthermore, he finds himself confronted with a curious paradox. When the patient has exposed the bizarre vicissitudes of his dream, when he has emphasized the unexpected nature of certain events in his nocturnal life, then the psychoanalyst, confident in his extensive culture, can say to him: "I know, I understand that; I expected as much. You are a man like any other. In spite of all the aberrations of your dream, you are not privileged with a singular existence."

And then it is the psychoanalyst who is charged with setting forth the *cogito* of the dreamer by saying: "He dreams at night; therefore, he exists at night. He dreams like everyone else; therefor, he exists like everyone else."

"He believes that he is himself during the night and he is just anybody."

"Just anybody? Or perhaps—disaster of the human being—anything?"

---

dream; there are no ordinary oneiric images. All the adjectives in a nocturnal dream are qualifiers. The philosopher who believes he can include the dream in thought would have a great deal of difficulty, while remaining in the world of dream, passing, as he does so easily in his lucid meditations, from the *whatever* to the *someone*.

Anything? Some surge of warm blood, some excessive hormone which has lost its organic wisdom.

Anything coming from any time? Some too scanty milk in the bottles of long ago.

The psychic substance examined by the psychoanalyst would then appear as a sum total of accidents. It would also remain impregnated by the dreams of long ago. On the mode of the *cogito,* the psychoanalyst-philosopher should say: "I dream; therefore I am dreaming substance." Dreams would then be that which roots itself the most deeply in the dreaming substance. Thoughts can be contradicted and, consequently, obliterated. But dreams? Dreams of the dreaming substance?

Then—let us ask once more—where do we place the *I* in this dreaming substance? Within it, the *I* dissolves and is lost. . . . Within it the *I* lends itself to supporting accidents after their validity has lapsed. In the nocturnal dream, the *cogito* of the dreamer stammers. The nocturnal dream does not even help us formulate a *non-cogito* which would express a sense of our will to sleep. It is this *non-cogito* which a metaphysics of the night should associate with losses of being.

In short, the psychoanalyst thinks too much. He does not dream enough. In wanting to explain to us the depth of our being by the residues deposited on the surface by daytime life, he obliterates the sense of the gulf that is within us. Who will help us descend into our caverns? Who will help us recover, recognize, know our double being which, from one night to the next, keeps us in existence. That sleepwalker who does not tramp along the routes of life but who descends, always descends in quest of immemorial resting places.

In its depths, the nocturnal dream is an ontological mystery. Whatever can be the being of a dreamer who, in the depth of his night, believes he is still living, who believes he is still the being of the semblances of life? Whoever loses some of his being is mistaken about his being. Even in the bright life, the subject of the verb "to be mistaken" is difficult to stabilize. In the abyssmal dream are there not nights when the dreamer takes the wrong abyss? Does he descend into himself? Does he go beyond himself?

Yes, there are nothing but questions at the threshold of a metaphysics of the night.

Before going so far, it will perhaps be necessary to study descents into the less-than-being (*moins-être*) in a realm which is more accessible than the dream of the nocturnal psyche. This is the problem we wish to reflect upon, by dealing simply with the *cogito* of reverie and not with a *cogito* of the nocturnal dream.

II

If the "subject" who dreams the nocturnal dream escapes us, if it is better grasped objectively by those who reconstitute it by analyzing the accounts of it made by the dreamer, the phenomenologist cannot work on the documents of nocturnal dreams. He must leave the study of the nocturnal dream to the psychoanalyst, or to the anthropologist who will compare the nocturnal dream to myths. All these studies will bring to light the immobile, anonymous man, the untransformable man which our phenomenological point of view leads us to call the man without a subject.

From then on, it is not by studying the nocturnal dream that we will be able to divulge the attempts at individualization which animate the man who is awake, the man whom ideas awaken, the man whose imagination calls him to subtlety.

Thus, since we wish to touch the poetic powers of the human psychism, it is best to concentrate all our research on simple reverie, by trying to determine clearly the specificity of simple reveries.

And here is the radical difference for us between the nocturnal dream (*rêve*) and reverie, the radical difference, a difference deriving from phenomenology; while the dreamer of the nocturnal dream is a shadow who has lost his self (*moi*), the dreamer of reverie, if he is a bit philosophical, can formulate a *cogito* at the center of his dreaming self (*son moi rêveur*). Put another way, reverie is an oneiric activity in which a glimmer of consciousness subsists. The dreamer of reverie is present in his reverie. Even when the reverie gives the impression of a flight out of the real, out of time and place, the dreamer of reverie knows that it is he who is absenting himself—he, in flesh and blood, who is becoming a "spirit," a phantom of the past or of voyage.

It will be easy for people to object to us that there is a whole range of intermediary states which go from rather clear reveries to formless musings (*rêvasseries*). Through this confused zone, phantasms lead us imperceptibly from day toward the night, from sleepiness to sleep. But is it self-evident that one falls from reverie into dream (*rêve*)? Are there really dreams which *continue* reveries? If the dreamer of reverie lets himself be overcome by sleepiness, his reverie unravels; it goes and gets lost in the sands of sleep, like streams in the desert. The place is free for a new dream, a dream which, like all nocturnal dreams, has an abrupt beginning. In going from reverie to dream, the sleeper crosses a frontier. And the dream is so new that the dream tellers rarely have confidence in an antecedent reverie.

But it is not in the realm of facts that we shall find an answer to the objection of a continuity from reverie to dream. We shall first have recourse to phenomenological principles. In fact, phenomenologically speaking, that is to say in taking the phenomenological examination to be linked, by definition, to any awareness (*prise de conscience*), we must repeat that a consciousness which is growing dark, diminishing and going to sleep has already ceased to be a consciousness. The reveries of the going-to-sleep are *facts*. The subject who submits to them has left the realm of *psychological* values. So we have a perfect right to neglect reveries which go down the wrong slope and reserve our research for the reveries which keep us in a consciousness of ourselves.

The reverie is going to be born naturally, in an awareness without tension, in an easy *cogito*, providing certainties of being with regard to a pleasing image—an image which pleases us because we have just created it, outside all responsibility, in the absolute liberty of reverie. The imagining consciousness holds its object (such images as it imagines) in an absolute immediacy. In a fine article which appeared in *Médecine de France*, Jean Delay uses the term *psychotrope* "to designate the group of chemical substances, whether of natural or artificial origin, which have a psychological tropism, that is to say, which are susceptible to modifying mental activity. . . . Thanks to the progress of psychopharmacology, medical workers have at their disposal today a great variety of psychotropic drugs allowing them to vary psychological behavior in different ways and to institute at will a regimen of relaxation, stimulation, dream or deliruim." [3] But if the carefully chosen substance causes psychotropisms, it is because there are psychotropisms. And a highly skilled psychologist could make use of psychotropic images. For there are psychotropic images which stimulate the psychism by inspiriting it into a sustained movement. The psychotropic image puts a little linear order into the psychic chaos. Psychic chaos is the state of the idle psyche, the less-than-being (*moins-être*) of the dreamer without images. The pharmaceutics of the milligram then come to enrich this latent psychism.

Confronted with such a success, an efficient dreamer (*songeur*) cannot stop short. The chemical substance brings the image. But wouldn't whoever brings us the image, the image alone, be giving us all the benefits of the substance? *In the psychological order, simulating the effect well is being very close to bringing back the cause.* The being of the dreamer of reverie is constituted by the images he conjures up. The image awakens us from our torpor, and our awakening is announced in a *cogito*. One more valorization, and there we are in the presence of positive reverie, a reverie which produces, a reverie which, however weak its product, can well be named poetic reverie. In its products and in its producer, reverie can well take on the etymological sense of the word "poetic." Reverie assembles being around its dreamer. It gives him illusions of being more than he is. Thus, upon this less-than-being (*moins-être*) which is the relaxed state where the reverie takes form, there emerges an outline in relief—a relief which the poet will know how to swell into a more-than-being. The philosophical study of reverie calls us to nuances of ontology.[4]

And this ontology is easy, for it is the ontology of well-being (*bien-être*)—of a well-being made to measure for the being of the dreamer who knows how to dream it. There is no well-being

---

3 Jean Delay, "Ten Years of Psycho-Pharmaceutics in Psychiatry," in *Médecine de France*. Paris, Oliver Perrin, p. 19.
4 I am nostalgic for remedies with beautiful names. Only a hundred years ago, there were such beautiful sentences in medicine. When the doctor knew how "to throw some vehicle in the humors," the sick person understood that he was going to be animated.

without reverie. No reverie without well-being. Already, through reverie, one discovers that being is a possession (*bien*). A philosopher will say that being is a value.

Must we forbid ourselves that summary characterization of reverie as happiness under the pretext that happiness is psychologically a flat, poor, puerile state—under the pretext too that just the word "happiness" extinguishes all analysis, drowns the psychism in banality? Poets—we shall quote some soon—will bring us the *nuances* of a cosmic happiness, nuances so numerous and so diverse that it will be fairly necessary to say that the world of reverie begins with the nuance. And thus it is that the dreamer of reverie gets an impression of originality. With the nuance, one comprehends that the dreamer knows the *cogito* being born.

The *cogito* which thinks can wander, wait, choose—the *cogito* of reverie is immediately attached to its object, to its image. The shortest route of all is between the imagining subject and the imagined image. Reverie lives from its primary interest. The subject of the reverie is astonished to receive the image, astonished, charmed, awakened. Great dreamers are masters of the glittering consciousness. A sort of multiple *cogito* renews itself in the closed world of a poem. Other consciential powers will, of course, be necessary in order to take possession of the poem in its totality. But already in the flash of an image, we find an illumination. What a lot of stippled reveries come to enhance the dreaming state! Aren't two types of reverie possible according to whether one lets himself flow into the succession of happy images or whether he lives at the center of an image while feeling it radiate? A *cogito* is assured in the soul of the dreamer who lives at the center of a radiating image.

III

Suddenly an image situates itself in the center of our imagining being. It retains us; it engages us. It infuses us with being. The *cogito* is conquered through an object of the world, an object which, all by itself, represents the world. The imagined detail is a sharp point which penetrates the dreamer; it excites in him a concrete meditation. Its being is at the same time being of the image and being of adherence to the image which is astonishing.

The image brings us an illustration of our astonishment. Perceptible registers correspond to each other. They complement each other. In a reverie which is dreaming on a simple object, we know a polyvalence of our dreaming being.

A flower, a fruit, or a simple, familiar object suddenly comes to solicit us to think of it, to dream near it, to help it raise itself to the rank of companion to man. Without the poets we would not know precisely how to find direct complements for our dreamer's *cogito*. Not all the objects of the world are available for poetic reveries. But once a poet has chosen his object, the object itself changes its being. It is promoted to the poetic.

What joy there is then in taking the poet at his word, in dreaming with him, in believing what he says, in living in the world he offers us by putting the world under the sign of the object, of a fruit of the world, or a flower of the world!

IV

The beginning of life is the beginning of a dream; thus Pierre Albert-Birot suggests that we live the happiness of Adam: "I feel that the world enters me like the fruits I eat; yes, truly, I nourish myself with the World." [5] Each fruit well tasted, each fruit poetically exalted is a type of happy world. And while dreaming well, the dreamer knows that he is a dreamer of the goods (*biens*) of the world, of the *closest* goods that the world offers him.

Fruits and flowers are already living in the being of the dreamer. Francis Jammes knew that: "I can scarcely feel any sentiment which is not accompanied by the image of a flower or a fruit." [6]

Thanks to a fruit, the whole being of the dreamer becomes round. Thanks to a flower, the whole being of the dreamer relaxes. Yes, what relaxation for the being in this single line by Edmond Vandercammen: "I spy a flower, adorable leisure . . ." [7] The flower born in poetic reverie, then, is the very being of the dreamer, his flowering being. The poetic garden dominates all

---

[5] Pierre Albert-Birot, *Mémoires d'Adam*, p. 126.
[6] Francis Jammes, *Le roman du lièvre*, appended notes, p. 271.
[7] Edmond Vandercammen, *L'étoile du berger*, p. 15.

the gardens of the earth. In no garden of the world could one pick this carnation, Anne-Marie de Backer's carnation:

> He left me all I need to live
> His black carnations and his honey in my blood.[8]

A psychoanalyst will quickly diabolize these two lines. But will he tell us that immense fragrance of a poet's flower which impregnates a whole life? And that honey—the incorruptible being—associated with the fragrance of blackness retained by the carnations, who will tell us how it keeps the dreamer alive? Upon reading such poems in complete sympathy, one feels that a past of what *could have been* is united with a past of what was:

> Abortive memories are worse than necessary
> They talk endlessly to invent life.

Thus the images of the poet's reverie dig life deeper, enlarge the depths of life. Let us pick that flower once again in the psychic garden: "The silver peony sheds its petals in the depths of fables." [9] To what depths of psychic reality the surrealism of women descends!

Flowers and fruits, beauties of the world; in order to be dreamed well, they must be spoken and spoken well. The dreamer of objects only finds the accents of ephemeral enthusiasm. What support he receives when the poet tells him: "You have seen well; therefore you have the right to dream." Then, hearing the voice of the poet, he enters the chorus of the "celebration." The celebrated beings are promoted to a new dignity of existence. Let us listen to Rilke "celebrate" the apple:

> Dare to speak what you call apple.
> That softness which first condenses
> In order, with a softness set up in the taste,
>
> to reach clarity, alertness, transparency,
> to become a thing of this place which means
> both the sun and the earth—[10]

---

8 Anne-Marie de Backer, *Les étoiles de novembre*, p. 16.
9 Anne-Marie de Backer, *loc. cit.*, p. 19.
10 Rilke, *Sonnets à Orphée*, I, no. XIII, in *Les élégies de Duino et les sonnets à Orphée*, translated by Angelloz. Aubier, 1943, p. 167.

Here, the translator found himself confronted with such a condensation of poetry that, with our analytical language, he had to disperse it a little. But the centers of condensation remain. The softness "set up in the taste" concentrates a softness of the world. The fruit that one holds in his hand gives a pledge of its ripeness. Its ripeness is transparent. Ripeness, the time economized for the benefit of one hour. What a lot of promises there are in a single fruit which joins the double sign of the sunny sky and the patient earth. The poet's garden is a fabulous garden. A past of legends opens a thousand paths to reverie. Avenues of the universe radiate out from the "celebrated" object. The apple celebrated by the poet is the center of a cosmos, a cosmos where the living is good, where one is sure of living. "All the fruits of the appletree are rising suns," says another poet to "celebrate" the apple.[11]

In another sonnet to Orpheus, the orange is the center of the world, a center of dynamism which transmits movements, frenzies and exuberances; for the maxim for life which Rilke proposes to us here is "Dance the orange" (*Tanzt die Orange*):

> Dance the orange. The warmest countryside,
> Project it out from you, that it may radiate ripeness
> in the air of its land! . . .[12]

Young girls must be the ones to "dance the orange," being light like perfumes. Perfumes! memories of the native atmosphere.

For Rilke, the apple and the orange are, as he says of the rose, "inexhaustible objects." [13] "Inexhaustible object" is truly the sign of the object that the poet's reverie makes emerge from its objective inertia! The poetic reverie is always new before the object to which it attaches itself. From one reverie to the next, the object is no longer the same; it renews itself and this renewing is a renewal of the dreamer. Angelloz gives an extensive commentary of the sonnet which "celebrates" the orange." [14] He situates it under the influence of Paul Valéry's *The Soul and the Dance* (the dancing lady is "the pure act of metamorphoses"); also under the influ-

11 Alain Bosquet, *Premier Testament*, p. 26.
12 *Sonnets I*, no. XV, translated by Angelloz, p. 171.
13 *Sonnets II*, no. VI, *loc. cit.*, p. 205.
14 Rilke, *loc. cit.*, p. 226.

ence of passages André Gide wrote in *Fruits of the Earth* on "The round of the pomegranate."

In spite of an inopportune point, the pomegranate, like the apple, like the orange, is round.

The beauty (*beauté*, f.) of the fruit is rounder the more it is sure of its feminine powers. What a reinforcement of pleasure for us when we dream all these reveries in *anima!*

At any rate, when one reads such poems, he feels himself in a state of *open symbolism*. Immobile heraldry can only retain antiquated aesthetic values. To dream of them well, it would be necessary to be unfaithful to the emblems. In front of the flower of fruit, the poet returns us to the birth of a happiness. And there precisely, Rilke finds "the happiness of eternal childhood":

> See the flowers, the faithful of the earth
> He who would carry them away into the
> intimacy of sleep and would sleep
> deeply with things—: O how light he would return
> different in the face of a different day, from
> the common depth.[15]

For the great renewing, it would doubtless be necessary to carry the flowers away into our dreams of the night. But the poet shows us that flowers are already coordinating generalized images in reverie. Not simply perceptual images, colors and fragrances, but images of man, of the delicacies of feeling, of warmths of memory, of temptations to make an offering, everything that can flower in a human soul.

Faced with this extravagance of fruits which invites us to taste the world, faced with those World-Fruits which solicit our reveries, how is it possible not to affirm that the man of reverie is cosmically happy. A type of happiness corresponds to each image. You cannot say of the man of reverie that he is "thrown to the world." For him the world is all welcome, and he himself is the principle of welcome. The man of reverie bathes in the happiness of dreaming the world, bathes in the well-being of a happy world.

---

[15] *Sonnets à Orphée*, II, no. XIV, *loc. cit.*, p. 221.

The dreamer is the double consciousness of his well-being and of the happy world. His *cogito* is not divided into the dialectic of subject and object.

The correlation between the dreamer and his world is a strong correlation. It is this world experienced through reverie which refers most directly back to the being of the solitary man. The solitary man directly possesses the worlds which he dreams. It is necessary not to dream if one is to doubt the worlds of reverie; it is necessary to come out of the reverie. The man of reverie and the world of his reverie are as close as possible; they are touching; they interpenetrate. They are on the same plane of being; if the being of man must be linked to the being of the world, the *cogito* of reverie will be expressed in the following manner: I dream the world, therefore, the world exists as I dream it.

Here there appears a privilege of poetic reverie. It seems that in dreaming in such solitude we can touch only a world so singular that it is foreign to every other dreamer. But the isolation is not so great, and the deepest, most particular reveries are often communicable. At least, there are families of dreamers whose reveries grow firm, whose reveries deepen the being which receives them. And thus it is that great poets teach us to dream. They nourish us with images with which we can concentrate our reveries of repose. They present us with their psychotropic images by which we animate an awakened oneirism. In such encounters, a Poetics of Reverie becomes conscious of its tasks: causing consolidations of imagined worlds, developing the audacity of constructive reverie, affirming itself in a dreamer's clear consciousness, coordinating liberties, finding some true thing in all the indisciplines of language, opening all the prisons of the being so that the human possesses all becomings. Those are just so many often contradictory tasks lying between what concentrates the being and what exalts it.

V

Of course, the Poetics of Reverie which we are outlining is in no way a Poetics of Poetry. The documentation on the awakened oneirism with which reverie provides us must be worked on— often worked on at length—by the poet in order to take on the dignity of poems. But, in the end, those documents formed by reverie are the most propitious matter to fashion into poems.

For those of us who are not poets, it is one of the access routes to poetry. Poets help us channel the flowing substance of our dreams (*songes*) and maintain it in a movement which adheres to laws. The poet retains the consciousness of dreaming distinctly enough to manage the task of writing his reverie. What a promotion of being it is to make a work out of a reverie, to be an author in reverie itself!

What relief is given to our language by a poetic image! If we could speak his high language and rise with the poet into that solitude of the speaking being who gives a new sense to the words of the tribe, we would be in a realm which is not entered by the active man for whom the man of reverie "is nothing but a dreamer" and for whom the world of reverie "is only a dream."

Of what importance to us, the dream (*songe*) philosopher, are those denials of the man coming back after his dream (*rêve*) to objects and men! The reverie *has been* a real state in spite of the illusions denounced after the event. And I am sure that I was the dreamer. I was there when all those beautiful things were present in my reverie. Those illusions were beautiful, and therefore beneficial. The poetic expression gained in the reverie adds to the richness of the language. Of course, if one analyzes the illusions by means of concepts, they will disperse at the first impact. But are there still, in this century, professors of rhetoric who analyze poems with ideas?

In any case, by looking a little, a psychologist always finds a reverie beneath a poem. Is it the poet's reverie? One is never sure, but by loving the poem, he sets about giving it oneiric roots, and thus it is that poetry nourishes within us reveries which we have not been able to express.

The fact will always remain that reverie is an original peace. Poets know it. Poets tell it to us. By a poem's exploit, reverie goes from a nirvana to poetic peace. In a book on Stefan George, Henry Benrath wrote: "Every creation springs from a sort of psychic nirvana." [16] It is through reverie, in an awakened oneirism,

---

[16] Henry Benrath, *Stefan George*, p. 27.

without going as far as nirvana, that many poets feel the forces of production fall into place. Reverie is that simple state where the work takes on its convictions by itself without being tormented by censorship. And thus it is that for many writers and poets the liberty of reverie opens paths to the work: "It is a bizarre disposition of my mind," writes Julien Green, "to believe a thing only if I have dreamed it. By believing, I do not mean simply possessing a certainty, but retaining it within oneself in such a way that the being finds itself modified because of it." [17] What a beautiful text for a philosophy of reverie is the one which says that the dream coordinates life, prepares beliefs for a lifetime.

The poet Gilbert Trolliet entitles one of his poems "Everything is Dreamed First" and he writes:

I wait. Everything is repose. Then innervated future
You are image within me. Everything is dreamed first.[18]

Thus creative reverie animates the nerves of the future. Nerve waves run along the lines of images shaped by reveries.[19]

In a passage from *The Antiquary*, Henri Bosco gives us a beautiful document which ought to help us prove that reverie is the *materia prima* of a literary work. The forms taken from the real need to be inflated with oneiric matter. The writer shows us the cooperation of the psychic reality function with the function of the unreal. In Bosco's novel, a character is speaking, but when a writer reaches that depth and lucidity at the same time, one can make no mistake about the intimacy of the confidence: "No doubt that in that singular time of my youth, what I was living, I thought I was dreaming and what I was dreaming, I thought I was living it. . . . Very often, those two worlds (of the real and the dream) interpenetrated and, without my knowing it, created a third equivocal world for me between reality and

---

[17] Julien Green, *L'aube vermeille*, 1950, p. 73. The psychiatrist J. H. Van den Berg took the Green quotation as an exergue for a study of Robert Desoille, *Evolution psychiatrique*, no. 1, 1952.
[18] Gilbert Trolliet, *La bonne fortune*, p. 61.
[19] In going beyond all human destiny, a visionary like Blake could say: "Everything which exists today was imagined long ago." And it is Paul Eluard who refers back to this absolute of the imagination (Paul Eluard, *Sentiers . . .*, p. 46).

dream (*songe*). Sometimes the most evident reality would melt into the mists there while a strangely bizarre fiction would illuminate my mind and make it marvelously subtle and lucid. Then the vague mental images would condense in such a way that one would have thought it possible to touch them with his finger. Tangible objects, on the other hand, would become phantoms of themselves, and I wouldn't be far from believing that one could pass through them as easily as he cuts through walls when he is walking around in dreams. When everything was back in order, I would get no other indication of it than a sudden and extraordinary faculty for loving noises, voices, fragrances, movements, colors and forms, which all of a sudden became perceptible in another way and yet with a familiar presence which delighted me." [20]

What an invitation to dream what one sees and to dream what one is. The dreamer's *cogito* moves off and goes to lend its being to things, to noises and to fragrances. Who is existing? What a relaxation for our own existence!

In order to have the sedative benefits of such a passage, it is necessary to read it *in slow reading*. We *understand* it too quickly (the writer is so clear!). We forget to dream it as it has been dreamed. In dreaming now, in a slow reading, we are going to believe in it, we are going to profit from it as from a gift of youth, to put our reverie youth into it, for we too, in the past, thought we were living what we were dreaming. . . . If we accept the hypnotic action of the poet's passage, our dreaming being will be returned to us from distant memory. A sort of *psychological memory*, calling an ancient Psyche back to life, calling back the very being of the dreamer we were, sustains our reading reverie. The book has just spoken to us of ourselves.

VI

The psychiatrist has doubtless encountered the phantomalization of familiar objects in numerous patients. But in his objective relationships, the psychiatrist, unlike the writer, does not help us make the phantoms *our* phantoms. Taken from the documents of

[20] Henri Bosco, *L'antiquaire*, p. 143.

the analysts, phantoms are only *hardened mists* offered to *perception*. Having named them, the analyst does not have to describe to us how these phantoms participate in our imagination through their intimate substance. On the contrary, the phantoms which take form in the writer's reverie are our intercessors to teach us to sojourn in the double life, at the sensitized frontier between the real and the imaginary.

A *poetic* force leads these phantoms of reverie. This poetic force animates all the senses; reverie becomes polysensorial. From the poetic passage, we receive a renewal of the joy of perceiving, a subtlety of all the senses—a subtlety which bears the privilege of a perception from one sense to another, in a sort of aroused Baudelarian correspondence. Awakening and no longer soporific correspondences. Ah! how a passage which pleases us can make us live! Thus in reading Bosco, one learns that the poorest objects are sachets of perfume, that, at certain times, internal lights render opaque bodies translucent, that every sonority is a voice. How the cup from which one drank as a child rings! From all over, coming from all objects, an intimacy lays siege to us. Yes, truly we dream while reading. The reverie which works poetically maintains us in an intimate space which does not stop at any frontier—a space uniting the intimacy of our being which dreams with the intimacy of the beings which we dream. It is within these composite intimacies that a poetics of reverie is coordinated. The whole being of the world is amassed poetically around the *cogito* of the dreamer.

On the contrary, active life, the life given animation by the reality function is a fragmented life, fragmenting outside us and within us. It rejects us to the exterior of all things. Then we are always *outside*. Always opposite things, opposite the world, opposite men with their mottled humanity. Except in the great days of true loves, except in the times of Novalis' *Umarmung*, a man is a surface for man. Man hides his depths. He becomes, as in Carlyle's parody, the consciousness of his clothes. His *cogito* assures his existence only within a mode of existence. And thus through artificial doubts, doubts in which—if it dare be said—he does not believe, he establishes himself as a thinker.

The dreamer's *cogito* does not follow such complicated preambles. It is easy; it is sincere; it is linked very naturally to its complementary object. Good things, soft things offer themselves in complete innocence to the innocent dreamer. And the dreams (*songes*) accumulate in front of a familiar object. The object is then the reverie companion of the dreamer. Easy certainties come to enrich the dreamer. A communication of being develops in both directions between the dreamer and his world. A great dreamer of objects like Jean Follain knows those hours when reverie becomes animated in an undulating ontology. An ontology with two united poles reverberates its certainties. The dreamer would be too much alone if the familiar object did not welcome his reverie. Jean Follain writes:

> In the closed up house
> he focuses on an object in the evening
> and plays that game of existing.[21]

In "that game of existing" how well the poet plays! He indicates his existence to the object on the table, to an infinitesimal detail which gives existence to a thing:

> The least crack
> in a windowpane or a bowl
> can bring back the felicity of a great memory
> the naked objects
> show their fine line
> sparkle all of a sudden
> in the sun
> but lost in the night
> gorge themselves as well on hours
> long
> or short.[22]

What a poem of tranquility! Say it slowly; there will descend within you an *object time*. How the object we dream helps us forget time and be at peace with ourselves! Alone "in the shut up house" with an object chosen to be a companion in solitude what assurance we have of being in simple existence! There will come

---

[21] Jean Follain, *Territoires*, p. 70.
[22] Jean Follain, *loc. cit.*, p. 15.

other reveries which, like those of a painter who likes to live the object in its ever particular appearances, will be able to return the dreamer to the picturesque life, other reveries too which will come from very distant memories. But an attraction to a completely simple presence calls the object dreamer to a sub-human existence. The eyes of Bérénice's ass gave Maurice Barrès such dreams (*songes*). But the sensitivity of the dreamers of looking (*rêveurs du regard*) is so great that everything which looks comes (up) to the level of the human. An inanimate object opens itself to the greatest dreams (*songes*). The sub-human reverie which equalizes the dreamer and the object becomes a sub-living reverie. To live this non-life is to carry to extremes "the game of existing" where Follain leads us on the gentle slope of his poems.

Object reveries sensitized to that extent lead us to reverberate to the object drama suggested to us by the poet:

> When there falls from the hands of the serving girl
> the pale round plate
> the color of the clouds
> the pieces must be picked up
> while the chandelier trembles
> in the masters' dining room.[23]

That it is pale and round, that it is the color of the clouds, in the prestige of these simple words poetically united, the plate takes on a poetic existence. It is not described, and yet whoever dreams a little will not confuse it with any other. For me it is the Jean Follain plate. Such a poem could be a test of the adherence of ordinary life to poetry. What solidarity exists between the beings of that house! With what human pity the poet can inspire the chandelier who trembles at the death of a plate! What a magnetic field there is between the servant and the masters, between the plate and the crystal of the chandelier for measuring the humanity of the beings of the house, of all the beings, men and things. Helped by the poet, how well we awaken ourselves from the sleep of indifference! Yes, how can we remain indifferent in front of such an object? Why look farther when we can dream on the clouds of the sky by contemplating a plate?

---

[23] Jean Follain, *loc. cit.*, p. 30; this poem is entitled "The Plate."

In dreaming before an inert object, a poet will always find a drama of life and non-life:

> I am a gray pebble; I have no other titles
> I dream while hardening the dreams of my choice.[24]

It is up to the reader to attach his preamble of sorrows to this poem, to relive all the petty sorrows which make up the gray look, all the troubles which make a heart of stone. In this poem from the *Premier Testament,* the poet calls us to the courage which hardens life. Besides, Alain Bosquet knows that to tell man's whole being, it is necessary to exist as the stone and the wind:

> It is an honor to be the wind
> It is a happiness to be the stone.[25]

But are there "still lifes" for a dreamer of things? Can things which have been human be indifferent? Don't things which have been named come back to life in the reverie on their name? Everything depends upon the dreaming sensitivity of the dreamer. Chesterton writes: "Dead things have such a power for taking over the living mind that I wonder if it is possible for anyone to read the catalogue of an auction without coming across things which, when abruptly recognized, would make elementary tears flow." [26]

Only reverie can awaken such a sensitivity. Dispersed at auction, offered to any taker, won't each gentle thing find its dreamer? A good writer from Champagne, the Trojan Grosley, said that his grandmother, when she did not know how to answer his childhood questions, would add: "Go on with you, when you're big, you will see that there are a lot of things in a *chosier.*"

But is our *chosier* really full? Isn't it rather encumbered with objects which do not bear witness to our intimacy? Our glass-doored whatnots are not really *chosiers* in the style of the grandmother from Champagne. Whenever someone curious comes into the parlor we exhibit our curios. Curios! just so many objects which do not speak their names immediately. We want them to

---

[24] Alain Bosquet, *Premier Testament.* Paris, Gallimard, p. 28.
[25] *Loc. cit.,* p. 52.
[26] G. K. Chesterton, *La vie de Robert Browning,* translation, p. 66.

be rare. They are samples of unknown universes. One must have "culture" in order to extricate himself from the middle of this bric-a-brac of sampled universes. To keep company with objects, there must not be too many. One does not dream well, in beneficial reveries, before dispersed objects. The object reverie is a faithfulness to the familiar object. The dreamer's faithfulness to his object is the condition for intimate reverie. The reverie maintains the familiarity.

A German author could somehow say: "Each new object, well considered, opens a new organ within us." (*Jeder neue Gegenstand, wohl beschaut, schliesst ein neues Organ in uns auf*). Things do not go so fast. It is necessary to dream a great deal in front of an object for the object to bring about within us a sort of oneiric organ. The objects privileged by reverie become the direct complements of the dreamer's *cogito*. They value the dreamer; they hold the dreamer. In the intimacy of the dreamer, then, they are the organs of reverie. We are not available for dreaming no matter what. If our object reveries are deep, they occur in the harmony between our oneiric organs and our *chosier*. Thus our *chosier* is precious to us, oneirically precious since it gives us the benefits of *attached reveries*. In such reveries, the dreamer recognizes himself as a dreaming subject. What a proof of being it is to recover both our I-dreamer (*moi-rêveur*) and the very object which is welcoming our reverie in a faithfulness of reverie. Those are connections of existences which one could not find in the meditation upon the nocturnal dream. The reverie dreamer's diffuse *cogito* receives from the objects of its reverie a tranquil confirmation of its existence.

VII

Philosophers of the strong ontology who overtake being in its totality and keep it integrally even in describing the most fleeting modes will quickly denounce this dispersed ontology which attaches itself to details, perhaps to accidents and which believes it is multiplying its proofs by multiplying its points of view.

But in the course of our life as a philosopher, we have insisted upon choosing subjects for our studies according to our capacities. And a philosophical study of reverie attracts us by its character which is both simple and well defined. Reverie is a manifest psychic activity. It contributes documentation on differences in the *tonality of the being*. At the level of the tonality of being a differential ontology can then be proposed. The dreamer's *cogito* is less lively than the thinker's *cogito*. The dreamers's *cogito* is less sure than the philosopher's *cogito*. The dreamer's being is a diffuse being. But on the other hand, this diffuse being is the being of a diffusion. It escapes the punctualization of the *hic* and of the *nunc*. The dreamer's being invades what it touches, diffuses into the world. Thanks to shadows, the intermediary region which separates man from the world is a full region, of a light density fullness. This intermediary region deadens the dialectic between being and non-being. The imagination does not know non-being. Its whole being can easily pass for a non-being in the eyes of the man at work, under the pen of the strong ontology metaphysician. But, on the other hand, the philosopher who gives himself enough solitude to enter the region of shadows bathes in an atmosphere without obstacles where no being says no. He lives by his reverie in a world homogenous with his being, with his demi-being. The man of reverie is always in space which has volume. Truly inhabiting the whole volume of his space, the man of reverie is from anywhere *in* his world, in an *inside* which has no *outside*. It is not without reason that people commonly say that the dreamer is *plunged* in his reverie. The world no longer poses any opposition to him. The I no longer opposes itself to the world. In reverie there is no more non-I. In reverie, the *no* no longer has any function: everything is welcome.

A philosopher enamored of the history of philosophy could say that the space in which the dreamer is plunged is a "plastic mediator" between man and the universe. It seems that in the intermediary world where reverie and reality mingle, a plasticity of man and his world is realized without one ever needing to know where the principle of this double malleability lies. This characteristic of reverie is so true that one can say, conversely, that where there is malleability, there is reverie. In solitude, it is enough that a dough be offered to our fingers to set us dreaming.[27]

---

[27] Cf. *La terre et les rêveries de la volonté*, ed. Corti, chap. IV.

Contrary to reverie, the nocturnal dream hardly knows this soft plasticity. Its space is encumbered with solids—and solids always have a reserve of sure hostility. They keep their forms and when a form appears, it is necessary to *think*, it is necessary to name. In the nocturnal dream, the dreamer suffers from a hard geometry. It is in the nocturnal dream that a pointed object wounds us as soon as we see it. In the nightmares of the night, objects are evil. A psychoanalysis which would work on the two shores, on the objective and the subjective sides, would recognize that the evil objects help us, one might say, to succeed in our "abortive acts." Our nightmares are often coordinations of abortive acts. They often make us live abortive lives. And how is it that psychoanalysis, so abundant in studies of dream-desire, has devoted so little space to the study of dream-remorse? The melancholy of certain of our reveries does not descend as far as those experienced, re-experienced misfortunes which a nocturnal dreamer can always dread reliving.

We cannot keep from ceaselessly renewing our efforts to indicate the difference between the night dream and the reverie of an alert consciousness. We are well aware that, by eliminating from our inquiries literary works which are inspired by nightmares, we are closing off perspectives directed at the human destiny and, at the same time, that we are depriving ourselves of the literary splendor of apocalyptic worlds. But we had to discard many problems if we wanted to treat the problem of the reverie of an awakened consciousness in all simplicity.

If this problem were clarified, perhaps the oneirism of the day could help us know the night oneirism better.

One would perceive that there are mixed states, reverie-dreams and dream-reveries—reveries which fall into dream and dreams which take on the color of reverie. Robert Desnos has pointed out that our nocturnal dreams are interrupted by simple reveries. In these reveries, our nights find gentleness again.

A wider inquiry than ours into the aesthetics of the oneirism should envisage a study of the artificial Paradises such as they have been described by writers and poets. What a lot of phenomenological ambitions would be necessary to uncover the "I" of different states corresponding to different narcotics! At the very least, it would be necessary to classify these "I's" in three species: the "I" of sleep—if it exists; the "I" of the narcosis—if it retains any value as individuality; the "I" of reverie, maintained in such vigilance that it can permit itself the happiness of writing.

Who will ever determine the ontological weight of all the imagined "I's"? A poet writes:

> This dream (*songe*) in us, is it ours
> I go alone and multiplied
> am I myself; am I another
> are we only imagined.[28]

Is there an "I" which assumes these multiple "I's"? An "I" of all these "I's" which has the mastery of our whole being, of all our intimate beings? Novalis writes: "Die höchste Aufgabe der Bildung ist, sich seines transzendantalen Selbst zu bemächtigen, das Ich seines Ichs zugleich zu sein." [29] If the "I's" vary in tonality of being, where is the dominant "I"? In looking for the "I" of the "I's" won't we find, by dreaming like Novalis, the "I" of the "I," the transcendental "I"?

But what are we looking for in the artificial Paradises—we who are only an armchair psychologist? Dreams or reveries? What are the determinant documents for us? Books, always books. Would the artificial Paradises be Paradises if they were not *written*? For us, as readers, these artificial Paradises are Paradises of reading.

The artificial Paradises were written to be read, with the certainty that the poetic value would provide the means of communication from the author to the reader. It is in order to write that so many poets have tried to live the reveries of opium. But who will tell us the respective roles of experience and art? On the subject of Edgar Allan Poe, Edmond Jaloux makes a penetrating remark. Edgar Allan Poe's opium is an *imagined opium*. Imagined before, reimagined after, but never written during. Who will show us the difference between experienced opium and magnified

[28] Leo Libbrecht, "Enchanteur de toi-même" in *Poemes choisis*, Paris, Seghers, p. 43.
[29] Novalis, *Schriften*, ed. Minor, 1907, vol. II, p. 117. "The supreme task of culture is to take possession of its transcendental self, to be at once the I of its I."

opium? We, the readers who do not wish to know, but wish to dream, we must follow the ascension which goes from the experience to the poem. "The power of man's imagination," concludes Edmond Jaloux, "is greater than all the poisons." [30] Edmond Jaloux says further in speaking of Edgar Allan Poe: "So he lends the poppy one of the most striking peculiarities of his own spirituality.[31]

But there too, can't the man who lives the psychotropic images find the impulsions of the psychotropic substance in them? The beauty of images adds to their effectiveness. The multiplicity of images relays the uniformity of the cause. A poet does not hesitate to give himself over entirely to the effectiveness of the image. Henri Michaux writes: "No need for opium. Everything is a drug for the man who chooses to live on the other side." [32]

And what is a beautiful poem if not a touched up madness? A little poetic order imposed upon aberrant images? The maintenance of an intelligent sobriety in the utilization—intensive all the same—of imaginary drugs. Reveries, mad reveries lead life.

---

30 Edmond Jaloux, *Edgar Poe et les femmes.* (Geneva, 1943), Ed. du Milieu du Monde, p. 125.
31 *Loc. cit.,* p. 129.
32 Henri Michaux, *Plume,* p. 68.

Five

Reverie and Cosmos

"The man who has a soul obeys only the universe."
> Gabriel Germain,
> *Chants pour l'âme d'Afrique*

"To define how Milosz thinks the world is to
paint the portrait of the pure poet of all time."
> Jean de Boschère,
> Preface to *Poèmes de O.V. de L. Milosz*

I inhabited a proverb so vast
that I needed the universe to fill it.
> Robert Sabatier,
> *Dédicace d'un navire*

I

When a dreamer of reveries has swept aside all the "preoccupa-tions" which were encumbering his everyday life, when he has detached himself from the worry which comes to him from the worry of others, when he is thus truly the *author of his solitude,* when he can finally contemplate a beautiful aspect of the uni-verse without counting the minutes, that dreamer feels a being opening within him. Suddenly such a dreamer is a *world dreamer.* He opens himself to the world, and the world opens itself to him. One has never seen the world well if he has not dreamed what he was seeing. In a reverie of solitude which in-creases the solitude of the dreamer, two depths pair off, reverber-ate in echoes which go from the depths of being of the world to a depth of being of the dreamer. Time is suspended. Time no longer has any yesterday and no longer any tomorrow. Time is engulfed in the double depth of the dreamer and the world. The World is so majestic that nothing any longer happens there; the World reposes in its tranquility. The dreamer is tranquil before a tranquil Water. Reverie can become deeper only by dreaming before a tranquil world. *Tranquility* is the very being both of the World and of its Dreamer. In his reverie of reveries, the philoso-pher knows an ontology of tranquility. Tranquility is the bond which unites the Dreamer and his World. In such a Peace there is established a psychology of capital letters. The dreamer's words become names of the World. They have access to the capital letter. Then the World is great, and the man who dreams it is a *Grandeur*. This grandeur in the image is often an objection for the man of reason. It would be enough for him if the poet would admit to a poetic intoxication. He would perhaps understand him by making the word "intoxication" abstract. But for the intoxication to be real, the poet drinks at the cup of the world. The metaphor is no longer enough for him; he needs the image. Here, for example, is the cosmic image of the magnified cup:

> In my horizon-edged cup
> I drink from the brim
> A simple swallow of sunshine
> Pale and icy.[1]

A critic who, parenthetically, is sympathetic to the poet, says that Pierre Chappuis' poem "bases its prestige upon the unexpected element of the metaphor and the unusual association of words." [2]

In his solitary reverie, the dreamer of cosmic reverie is the veritable subject of the verb "to contemplate," the primary evidence of the power of contemplation. The World is then the direct object of the verb "to contemplate." Is it *knowing* (*connaître*) to contemplate while dreaming? Is it *understanding*? It is certainly not *perceiving*. The eye which dreams does not see, or at least it sees with another vision. This vision is not constituted of "leftovers." Cosmic reverie makes us live in a state which must be designated as ante-perceptive. The communication between the dreamer and his world is very close in reverie; it has no "distance," not that distance which marks the *perceived world*, the world fragmented by perception. Of course, we are not speaking here of the post-perception reverie of lassitude, where lost perceptions grow dark. What becomes of the perceived image when the imagination takes over the image to make it the sign of

---

[1] Pierre Chappuis, from a poem published in the *Revue neuchâteloise*, March, 1959, entitled "A l'horizon tout est possible." Without taking the trouble to give us an image, Barrès was content to say that at the edge of the Italian lakes "one gets drunk 'at the cup of light' which is that countryside" (*Du sang, de la volupté et de la mort*. Paris, Albert Fontemoing, p. 174.) Chappuis' lines help me dream better in the majesty of the image, than too short a metaphor.

[2] Marc Eigeldinger, in *Revue neuchâteloise*, p. 19.

a world? In the poet's reverie, the world is imagined, directly imagined. There, we are touching on one of the paradoxes of the
imagination: while thinkers who reconstruct a world retrace a
long path of reflections, *the cosmic image is immediate*. It gives us
the whole before the parts. In its exuberance, it believes it is telling the whole of the Whole. It holds the universe with one of its
signs. A single image invades the whole universe. It diffuses
throughout the universe the happiness we have at inhabiting the
very world of that image. In his reverie without limit or reserve,
the dreamer gives himself over, body and soul, to the cosmic image which has just charmed him. The dreamer could not doubt
that he is in a world. A single, cosmic image gives him a unity of
reverie, a unity of world. Other images are born from the first
image, come together and mutually embellish each other. Never
do the images contradict each other; the world dreamer does not
know the division of his being. Before all the "openings" of the
world, the world thinker makes it a rule to hesitate. The world
thinker is the being of a hesitation. From the time of the opening
of the world through an image, the world *dreamer* inhabits the
world which has just been offered him. A universe can be born
from an isolated image. Once more we see the magnifying imagination in action following the rule set forth by Arp: "The little
holds the big on a leash." [3]

In the preceding chapter, we were indicating that a fruit by
itself was the promise of a world, an invitation to be in the world.
When the cosmic imagination works on this original image, it is
the world itself which is a gigantic fruit. The moon and the earth
are fruited stars. How else can we taste a poem like this one by
Jean Cayrol:

> O silence round like the earth
> movements of the mute Star
> gravitation of fruit around the clay nucleus. [4]

The world is thus dreamed in its roundness, in its fruitlike
roundness. Then happiness flows back from the world toward the

---

[3] Arp, *Le siège de l'air*, ed. Alain Gheerbrant, 1946, p. 75.
[4] Jean Cayrol, *Le miroir de la Rédemption du monde*, p. 25.

fruit. And the poet who has thought the world as a fruit can say:

> May no one wound the Fruit
> it is the past of joy which is becoming round.[5]

If in place of a book for leisure reading we were writing a thesis in aesthetic philosophy, we should at this time multiply the examples of this power of cosmicity of poetically privileged images. A particular cosmos forms around a particular image as soon as a poet gives the image a destiny of grandeur. The poet gives the real object its imaginary double, its idealized double. This idealized double is immediately idealizing, and it is thus that a universe is born from an expanding image.

II

In their magnification to the point of cosmic becoming, images are certainly units of reverie. But these units of reverie are so numerous that they are ephemeral. A more stable unit appears when a dreamer dreams of matter, when in his dreams (*songes*) he goes "to the bottom of things." Everything becomes great and stable at the same time when the reverie unifies cosmos and substance. In the course of interminable research on the imagination of the "four elements," on the substances which, since time immemorial, man has always imagined to sustain the unity of the world, we have very often dreamed upon the action of traditionally cosmic images. These images, taken at first very close to man, expand by themselves to the level of the universe. One dreams in front of his fire, and the imagination discovers that the fire is the motive force for a world. One dreams in front of a spring and the imagination discovers that water is the blood of the earth, that the earth has living depths. He has a soft, fragrant dough beneath his fingers and proceeds to knead the substance of the world.

Upon his return from such reveries, one hardly dares say he has dreamed that big. As the poet says, man, "no longer able to dream, thought." [6] And the world dreamer begins to think the

---

[5] *Loc. cit.,* p. 45.
[6] Ernest La Jeunesse, *L'imitation de notre maître Napoléon*, (Paris, 1897), p. 51.

world through the thought of others. Just the same, if one wishes to speak of those dreams (*songes*) which constantly return, living and active, he takes refuge in history, in a distant history, in a faraway history, in the history of forgotten cosmoseṣ. Haven't the philosophers of antiquity given us precise evidence of worlds substantialized by a cosmic substance? Those were *the dreams of great thinkers*. I am always astonished that historians of philosophy *think* these great cosmic images without ever *dreaming* them, without ever restoring to them their privilege of reverie. Dreaming reveries and thinking thoughts are certainly two disciplines which are hard to reconcile. At the end of a jostled culture, I believe more and more that they are the disciplines of two different lives. So it seems to me best to separate them and thus to break with the common opinion that believes that reverie leads to thought. The ancient cosmogonies do not give order to thoughts; they are audacious reveries, and in order to bring them back to life, it is necessary to learn to dream again. Today there are archaeologists who understand the oneirism of the original myths. When Charles Kerenyi writes: "Water is the most mythological of the elements," he is sensing that water is the element of the gentle oneirism. It is an exception that malevolent deities emerge from water. But in the present essay we are not utilizing mythological documents; we are envisaging only the reveries which we are able to relive.

Through the cosmicity of an image then, we receive an experience of the world; cosmic reverie causes us to inhabit a world. It gives the dreamer the impression of a *home* (*chez soi*) in the imagined universe. The imagined world gives us an expanding *home*, the reverse of the *home* of the bedroom. Victor Ségalen, the poet of voyage, said that the bedroom is "the goal of the returning." [7] In dreaming on the universe, one is always *departing*; one lives in the *elsewhere*—in an elsewhere which is always *comfortable*. To designate a dreamed world well, it is necessary to mark it with a happiness.

So we are always coming back upon our thesis that we must affirm in general and in detail that reverie is a consciousness of

[7] Victor Ségalen, "Equipée," *Voyage au pays du réel.* (Paris, 1929), Plon, p. 92.

well-being. In a cosmic image as well as in an image of our dwelling, we are in the well-being of a repose. The cosmic image gives us a concrete, specified repose; this repose corresponds to a need, to an appetite. The formula that the world is my appetite must be substituted for the philosopher's general formula that the world is my representation. To bite into the world with no other "care" than the happiness of biting, isn't that entering the world? What a grasp of the world is a bite. Then the world is the direct object of the verb "I eat." And thus it is that for Jean Wahl, the lamb is the direct object of the wolf. Commenting on the work of William Blake, the philosopher of being writes thusly: "The lamb and the tiger are one and the same being." [8] Tender flesh, strong teeth, what harmony, what unity of the total being!

Linking the world to man's need, Franz von Baader wrote: "The only possible proof of the existence of water, the most convincing and the most intimately true proof, is thirst." [9]

How can we say, in front of all the offerings which the World presents to man, that man is rejected by the World after first being thrown into the World?

For every appetite, there is a world. The dreamer then participates in the world by nourishing himself from one of the substances of the world, a dense or rare, warm or gentle substance clear or full of penumbra according to the *temperament of his imagination*. And when a poet comes to help the dreamer in renewing the beautiful images of the world, the dreamer accedes to cosmic health.

III

A diffused well-being emerges from the dream. Diffused-diffusing following the oneiric rule of the passage from the past

---

[8] Jean Wahl, *Pensée, Perception*. Calmann-Lévy, 1948, p. 218. And what a document for a metaphysics of the jawbone! One reads in Troubetzkoy's *Principes de phonologie*, translated, 1949, p. xxiii, note: "At the end of the last century, Martynov, a Russian lunatic, published a brochure entitled, *Découverte du mystère de la langue humaine en révélation de la faillite de la linguistique savante* where he tries to prove that all the words in human languages go back to roots meaning "to eat" (note by Jacobsen). Biting is certainly getting to the meat of things for participating in the world."

[9] E. Susini, *Franz von Baader et le romantisme mystique*, vol. I, p. 143.

participle to the present participle. The diffusing well-being transforms the world into "environment" (*milieu*). Let us give an example of this renewal of the cosmic health won by an adherence to an environment of the world. We shall take this example from the psychiatrist J. H. Schultz's method of "autogenous training." It is a question of teaching the anguished sick person the certainties of good breathing again: "In the states we are trying to induce, breathing very often becomes, according to the patients' accounts, a sort of *milieu* within which they stir. . . . Like a bark on a tranquil sea, I raise and lower myself while breathing. . . . In normal cases, it is sufficient to use the formula 'Breathe calmly.' The respiratory rhythm can acquire such a degree of *interior*[10] manifestness that one can say: "I am all breathing." [11]

The translator of Schultz's passage adds in a note: "This translation is but a feeble approximation of the German expression '*Es atmet mich*,' literally 'It breathes me.' In other words, the world comes to breathe within me; I participate in the good breathing of the world; I am plunged into a breathing world. Everything breathes in the world. The good breathing which is going to cure me of my asthma, of my anguish, is a cosmic breathing."

In one of his *Orientales*,[12] Mickiewicz tells the full life of the expanded chest: "Oh! How soft it is to breathe with all one's chest! I breathe freely, fully, widely. All the air of Arabistan is hardly enough for my lungs."

Jules Supervielle, poetically translating a poem by Jorge Guillen knows this breathing of the world:

> Air that I breathe deeply
> So many suns made it dense
> And, for more avidity
> Air where time is breathing.

---

10 Our italics.
11 J. H. Schultz, *Le training autogène*. Adaptation P.U.F., p. 37. Cf. G. Sand *Dernières pages:* "Une nuit d'hiver," p. 33:
"The air one takes in without paying attention and in thinking of other things does not vivify like the air one takes in for the taking in." In a thesis in medicine defended in Lyons in 1958, François Dagognet added many elements to a psychology of respiration. A chapter of this thesis was published in the review *Thalès*, 1960.
12 *Oeuvres traduites*, vol. I, p. 83.

In the happy human breast, the world breathes itself, time breathes itself. And the poem continues:

> I breathe, I breathe
> So deeply that I see myself
> Enjoying the paradise
> Par excellence, ours.[13]

A great breather like Goethe puts meteorology under the sign of respiration. In a cosmic respiration, the whole atmosphere is breathed by the earth. In a conversation with Eckermann, Goethe said: "I imagine the earth with its circle of vapors like a great living being which inhales and exhales eternally. If the earth inhales, it draws to it the circle of vapors which approaches its surface and thickens into clouds and rain. I call this state the *aqueous affirmation;* if it lasted beyond the prescribed time, it would drown the earth. But the earth does not permit that; it exhales again and sends back up the vapors of water which spread into all the spaces of the high atmosphere and thin out to such an extent that not only does the brilliance of the sun cross through them, but that the eternal night of infinite space, seen through them, is colored with a brilliant blue tint. I call this second state of the atmosphere the *aqueous negation.* In the state of aqueous negation, not only does no humidity arrive from above, but in addition the humidity of the earth . . . disappears into the air in such a way that if this state were prolonged beyond the prescribed time, even without sunlight, the earth would run the risk of drying up and becoming completely hard." [14]

When comparisons go that easily from man to the world, a reasonable philosopher posits, without risk of error, his diagnosis of anthropomorphism. The reasoning which supports the images is simple: since the earth is "living," it is self-evident that, like all living beings, it breathes. It breathes, as man breathes, by chasing its breath away from itself. But here it is Goethe who is speaking; it is Goethe who is reasoning; it is Goethe who is imagining. From that point on, if one wishes to reach the Goethean level, the direction of the comparison must be reversed. It would be too

---

13 Jules Supervielle, *Le corps tragique*, ed. Gallimard, pp. 122–123.
14 *Conversations de Goethe avec Eckermann*, translation, vol. I, p. 335.

little to say that the earth breathes as man does. One must say
that Goethe breathes as the earth breathes. Goethe breathes with
all his lungs as the earth breathes with all its atmosphere. The
man who reaches the glory of breathing breathes cosmically.[15]
The first sonnet in the second part of the *Sonnets to Orpheus* is a
sonnet on breathing, on a cosmic breathing:

> To breathe, o invisible poem!
> Pure exchange which never ends between our own being
> and the expanses of the world . . .
>
> Unique wave, of which
> I am the progressive sea;
> you, the most economical of all possible seas,
> gain of space.
>
> How many among those places of the expanses were already
> inside myself. More than one wind
> is like my son.[16]

The exchange of being goes that far in an equality of the being
who breathes and the breathed world. Wind, breezes, great gusts,
aren't they all the creatures, the sons of the breast of the poet who
is breathing?

And aren't the voice and the poem the respiration of the
dreamer and the world in common? Or so the last tercet pro-
claims;

> Do you recognize me, air, you, still full of
> places that were mine?
> You, who were once the smooth bark,
> the curve and the leaf of my words?

And how can one live anywhere but at the summit of the synthesis when the air of the world makes both the tree and the man
speak, mixing all the forests, those of the vegetable kingdom
along with those belonging to the poets?

---

15 Barrès who set himself the rule of "breathing with sensuality" (*Un homme
libre*, p. 234) would not have gone so far. By following a doctrine of imagination, on the contrary, much "outside" is necessary to cure a little "inside."
16 Rilke, *Les élégies de Duino. Les sonnets à Orphée*, translated by Angelloz, p. 195.

Thus poems come to our aid in finding the breathing of the great gusts again, the original breathing of the child who breathes the world. In my utopia of recovery through poetry, I would propose the meditation of this single line: "Canticle of childhood, O lungs of speech." [17]

What a magnification of breath there is when the lungs speak, sing, make poems! Poetry helps one breathe well.

Is it necessary to add that in poetic reverie, the triumph of calm, the summit of confidence in the world, one breathes well. What a reinforcement of efficiency the exercises in "autogenous training" would receive from the association of well chosen reveries with the exercises proposed by the psychiatrist. Schultz's patient did not bring up the tranquil bark without good reason, the bark, that cradle,[18] sleeping on waters which breathe.

It seems that such images, if they were well assembled, would give a supplementary efficiency to the good psychiatrist's contact with the patient.

IV

But our goal is not to study dreamers. We would die of boredom if we had to make inquiries among the companions in relaxation. We wish to study not the reverie which puts one to sleep but the *working reverie* (*rêverie oeuvrante*), the reverie which prepares works. Books, and no longer men, are then our documents, and our entire effort in reliving the poet's reverie is to feel its working (*oeuvrant*) character. Such poetic reveries give us access to a world of psychological values. Along the normal axis of cosmic reverie, the perceptible universe is transformed into a universe of beauty. Is it possible, *in a reverie,* to dream of ugliness, of an immobile ugliness that no light would correct? On this point, we are again touching the characteristic difference between the dream and reverie. Monsters belong to the night, to the nocturnal dream.[19] Monsters do not organize themselves into a mon-

---

17 Jean Laugier, *L'espace muet.* Paris, Seghers.
18 "Cradle" translates both "ce berceau" and "cette berce" (Translator's note).
19 Caricatures belong to the "mind." They are "social." Solitary reverie could not take pleasure in them.

strous universe. They are fragments of a universe. And, very exactly, in the cosmic reverie, the universe takes on a unity of beauty.

To deal with this problem of a cosmos given a value by a unity of beauty, how favorable the meditation of the work of painters would be! But as we believe that each art calls for a specific phenomenology, we want to present our observations by using literary documents, the only ones at our disposal. Let us simply note a sentence by Novalis which expresses, in a decisive manner, the active pancalism which animates the will of the painter at work. "The art of the painter is the art of seeing beautiful." [20]

But this will to see beautiful is taken over by the poet who must see beautiful in order to speak beautiful. There are poetic reveries where the look has become an activity. Following an expression which Barbey d'Aurevilly uses to tell of his victories over women, the painter knows how to "make himself some gaze" (*se faire du regard*) as the singer, in a long exercise, knows how to project his voice (*se faire de la voix*). Then the eye is no longer simply the center of a geometrical perspective. For the contemplator who "has made himself some gaze," the eye is the projector of a human force. A subjective, clarifying force comes to heighten the lights of the world. There exists a reverie of the lively look, a reverie which is animated in a pride of seeing, of seeing clearly, of seeing well, of seeing far, and this pride of vision is perhaps more accessible to the poet than to the painter: the painter must paint this super-elevated vision; the poet has only to proclaim it.

What a lot of texts we could quote which tell that the eye is a center of light, a little human sun which projects its light on the looked at object, well looked at in a will to see *clearly*.

A very curious text by Copernicus can, all by itself, help us posit a cosmology of light, an astronomy of light. Of the Sun, Copernicus, that reformer of astronomy, writes. "Some have called it the pupil (*prunelle*) of the world, others the Spirit (of the world), and yet others its Rector. Trismegistus calls it God visible. Sophocles' *Electra* calls it the all-seeing." [21] Thus planets

[20] Novalis, *Schriften*. ed. Minor, vol. II, p. 228.
[21] Copernicus, *Des révolutions des orbes célestes*. Introduction, translation and notes by A. Koyré. Paris, Alcan, p. 116.

turn around an Eye of Light and not a heavily attracting body. The gaze is a cosmic principle.

But our demonstration will perhaps be more decisive if we take more recent texts, more clearly marked by the pride of seeing. In an *Orientale* by Mickiewicz, a hero of vision exclaims: "I stared with pride at the stars which fixed on me their eyes of gold, for in the desert they saw only me alone." [22]

In an essay from his youth, Nietzsche wrote: " . . . the dawn ventures to confront the sky decorated with multiple colors . . . My eyes have an entirely different brilliance. I am afraid they will make holes in the sky." [23]

More contemplative, less aggressive is the cosmicity of the eye for Claudel: "We can," says the poet, "see in the eye a sort of scaled down, portable sun, and therefore, a prototype of the ability to establish a radius (*rayon*) from it to any point on the circumference." [24] The poet could not leave the word *"rayon"* [25] in its geometric tranquility. He had to give the word *"rayon"* back its solar reality. Then the eye of a poet is the center of a world, the sun of a world.

That which is round is very close to being an eye when the poet accepts the faint lunacies of poetry:

> O magic circle: eye of all being!
> Volcano eye shot with unhealthy blood
> Eye of that black lotus
> Arisen from the calm of the dream.

And Yvan Goll giving the sun-look its imperious power can write further:

> The universe revolves around you
> Eye with facets which chase away the eyes of the stars
> And implies them in your gyratory system
> Carrying away nebulas of eyes in your madness.[26]

---

22 Mickiewicz, *loc. cit.*, vol. I, p. 82.
23 Richard Blunck, *Frédéric Nietzsche. Enfance et jeunesse.* Translated by Eva Sauser (Paris, 1955), Corréa, p. 97.
24 Paul Claudel, *Art poétique*, p. 106.
25 The word *rayon* means both "radius" and "ray" (Translator's note).
26 Yvan Goll, *Les cercles magiques.* Paris, edit. Falaize, p. 45.

Being completely given over to our happy reveries, we are not tackling the psychology of the "bad eye" in this simple book. What a lot of research would be necessary to separate the bad eye against men from the bad eye against things! Whoever believes he has a power against men readily admits that he has a power against things. One finds the following note in the *Infernal Dictionary* by Collin de Plancy (p. 553): "In Italy there were witches who, with a single look, would eat the heart of men and the insides of cucumbers."

But the world dreamer does not regard the world as an object; the aggressiveness of the *penetrating* look is of no concern to him. He is the contemplating subject. It then seems that the contemplated world passes through a scale of clarity when the consciousness of seeing is the consciousness of seeing big and the consciousness of seeing beautiful. Beauty works actively on the perceptible. Beauty gives relief to the contemplated world and is an elevation in the dignity of seeing at the same time. When one agrees to follow the development of the aestheticizing psychology in the double valorization of the world and of its dreamer, it seems that one knows a communication of two principles of vision between the beautiful object and seeing it beautiful. Then in an exaltation of the happiness of seeing the beauty of the world, the dreamer believes that, between him and the world, there is an exchange of looks, as in the double look from the loved man to the loved woman. "The sky . . . seemed a great blue eye which was looking lovingly at the earth." [27] In order then to express the thesis of Novalis on an active pancalism, it would be necessary to say that everything I look at looks at me.

Gentleness of seeing while admiring, pride of being admired, those are human bonds. But they are active, in both directions, in our admiration of the world. The world wishes to see itself; the world lives in an active curiosity with ever open eyes. In uniting mythological dreams (*songes*), we can say: *The Cosmos is an Argus*. The Cosmos, a sum of beauties, is an Argus, a sum of ever open eyes. Thus the theorem of the reverie of vision is translated

---

[27] Théophile Gautier, *Nouvelles. Fortunio*, p. 94.

to the cosmic level: everything that shines sees, and there is nothing in the world which shines more than a look.

Water gives a thousand indications of the universe which sees, of the universe-argus. At the slightest breeze, the lake is covered with eyes. Each wave raises itself to see the dreamer better. Théodore de Banville could say: "There exists a frightening resemblance between the look of lakes and that of human pupils (*prunelles*)." [28] Must we give this "frightening resemblance" all its meaning? Did the poet know the *fright* which seizes a mirror dreamer when that dreamer feels himself being watched by himself? To be seen by all the mirrors of the lake ends up perhaps as an obsession with being seen. It was Alfred de Vigny, I believe, who noted the alarmed modesty of a woman who is suddenly aware that her dog has just looked at her while she was changing her slip.

But we shall come back later to this reversal of being that the dreamer brings to the world contemplated by the painter who sees beautiful. But from the world to the dreamer the reversal is still greater when the poet obliges the world to become, beyond even a world of the look, the *World of the word.*

In the world of the word, when the poet abandons signifying language for the poetic language, the aesthetization of the psychism becomes the dominant psychological sign. The reverie which wants to express itself becomes poetic reverie. It is along these lines that Novalis could say plainly that the liberation of the perceptible in a philosophical aesthetics would develop by following the scale: music, painting, poetry.

We are not taking up this hierarchy of arts as our own. For us all human summits are *summits.* The summits reveal to us marvels of the psychic novelties. By the poet, the world of the word is renewed in its principle. The true poet, at least, is bilingual; he does not confuse the language of meaning with poetic language. Translating one of these languages into the other could be no more than a poor trade.

The poet's exploit at the summit of his cosmic reverie is to

---

[28] *Revue fantastique*, vol. II, June 15, 1861, in an article devoted to Bresdin.

constitute a cosmos from the word.[29] What a lot of seductions the poet must link together in order to draw in an inert reader so that the reader may understand the world from the basis of the poet's praise! What an adherence to the world to live in the world of praise! Every beloved thing becomes the being of its praise. By loving the things of the world, one learns to praise the world: he enters into the cosmos of the word.

Then what a new company of the world and its dreamer! A spoken reverie transforms the solitary dreamer's solitude into a company open to all the beings of the world. The dreamer speaks to the world, and now the world is speaking to him. Just as the duality of the looked-at to the looking-at is magnified into a duality of the Cosmos to the Argus, the more subtle duality of the Voice and the Sound rises to the cosmic level of a duality of the breath and the wind. Where is the dominant being of the spoken reverie? When a dreamer speaks, who is speaking, he or the world?

Here we shall invoke one of the axioms of the Poetics of reverie, a veritable theorem which ought to convince us to link the Dreamer indissolubly with his World. We shall take this poetic theorem from a master in poetic reveries: "All the being of the world, if it dreams, dreams that it is speaking." [30]

But does the being of the world dream? Ah! long ago, before "culture," who would have doubted it? Everyone knew that metal ripened slowly in the mine. And how can anything ripen without dreaming? How can goods, forces and odors be amassed within a beautiful object of the world without accumulating dreams? And the earth—when it did not turn—how would it have ripened its seasons without dreams? The great dreams of cosmicity are guarantees of the immobility of the earth. Even if reason, after long work, comes to prove that the earth turns, it is no less true that such a declaration is *oneirically absurd*. Who

[29] "The image is formed of the words which dream it," says Edmond Jabès, *Les mots tracent*, p. 41.
[30] Henri Bosco, *L'antiquaire*, p. 121. And what pages (121–122) for the man who wants to understand that poetic reverie unites the dreamer and the world!

could *convince* a cosmos dreamer that the earth spins around upon itself and that it flies in the sky? One does not dream with taught ideas.[81]

Yes, before culture, the world dreamed a great deal. Myths came out of the earth, opened the earth so that, with the eye of its lakes, it looks at the sky. A destiny of height arose from the abysses. Thus the myths found men's voices immediately, the voice of man dreaming the world of his dreams. Man expressed the earth, the sky, the waters. Man was the word of his macroanthropos which is the monstrous body of the earth. In primitive cosmic reveries, the world is a human body, a human look, a human breath, a human voice.

But can't those times of the speaking world be reborn? Whoever goes to the bottom of reverie rediscovers natural reverie, a reverie of the original cosmos and the original dreamer. The world is no longer mute. Poetic reverie revives the world of original words. All the beings of the world begin to speak by the name they bear. Who has named them? The names are so well chosen that they seem to have named themselves. One word leads to another. The words of the world want to make sentences. The dreamer knows it well, that dreamer who makes an avalanche of words issue from a word that he dreams. The water which "is sleeping" all black in the pond, the fire which "is sleeping" beneath the ashes, all the air of the world which "is sleeping" in a fragrance—all these "sleeping beings" (*dormants*) bear witness, by sleeping so well, to an interminable dream. In the cosmic reverie, nothing is inert, neither the world nor the dreamer; everything lives with a secret life, so everything speaks sincerely. The poet listens and repeats. The voice of the poet is a voice of the world.

Naturally, we are free to rub our eyes and sweep away all these mad images, all these "reveries on reverie" of an idle philosopher. But then it is necessary not to read any further in the passage by Henri Bosco. It is necessary not to read the poets. In their cosmic reverie, poets speak of the world in original words, in original images. They speak of the world in the language of the world.

---

81 Musset writes (*Oeuvres posthumes*, p. 78): "The poet has never dreamed that the earth revolves around the sun."

Words, beautiful words, great natural words believe in the image which has created them. A word dreamer recognizes in a man's word applied to a thing of the world a sort of oneiric etymology. If there are "gorges" [32] in the mountains, isn't it because the wind, long ago, spoke there? [33] In *Monday Vacation,* Théophile Gautier hears "animalized" winds, "overworked elements, tired of their tasks," [34] in the mountain gorge. Thus there are cosmic words, words which give man's being to the being of things. And thus it is that the poet could say: "It is easier to include the universe in a word than in a sentence." [35] Through reverie, words become immense; they abandon their poor, original determinations. Thus, the poet finds the greatest, most cosmic of squares by writing: "O Great square which has no angles." [36]

Thus cosmic words, cosmic images weave bonds between man and the world. A light delirium makes the dreamer of cosmic reverie pass from a human vocabulary to a vocabulary of things. The two human and cosmic tonalities reinforce each other. For example, listening to the trees of the night prepare their tempests, the poet will say: "The forests shiver under the caresses of the cristal-fingered delirium." [37] That which is electric in the shiver—whether it runs along man's nerves or along the fibers of the forest—has met a sensitive detector in the poet's image. Don't such images bring us the revelation of a sort of intimate cosmicity? They unite the outside cosmos with an inside cosmos. Poetic exaltation—the crystal-handed delirium—makes an intimate forest shiver within us.

In cosmic images, it often seems that man's words infuse human

---

[32] *La gorge* in French means "gorge" and "throat" (Translator's note).

[33] Another bell for my fool's cap of the word dreamer: only a geographer who believes that words serve to describe "accidents" of terrain "objectively" can hold "gorge" and "narrows" (*étranglement*) to be synonyms. For a word dreamer of course, it is the feminine here which tells the human truth of the mountain. To express my attachment to hills, valleys, paths, groves, rocks, and grottos, I would have to write a "non-figurative" geography of names. In any case, this non-figurative geography is the geography of memories.

[34] Théophile Gautier, *Les vacances du lundi,* p. 306.

[35] Marcel Havrenne, *Pour une physique de l'écriture,* p. 12.

[36] Henry Bauchau, *Géologie,* Paris, Gallimard, p. 84.

[37] Pierre Reverdy, *Risques et périls,* p. 150. And in the same way (p. 157), Pierre Reverdy listens to the poplars which go so high to speak in the sky: "The poplars tremble gently in their mother tongue."

energy into the being of things. Here, for example, is the grass
saved from its humility by the corporal dynamism of a poet:

> Grass
> carries away the rain on its millions of backs,
> holds back the soil with its millions of toes.
>
> . . . .

The grass

> answers each menace by growing.
> Grass loves the world as much as itself,
> Grass is happy, whether times are hard or not,
> Grass passes rotted, grass wanders
> On its feet.[38]

Thus, the poet puts the bent-bending being *on its feet*.
Through him, greenery has energy. An appetite for life increases
through the ardor of words. The poet no longer describes; he exalts. He must be understood by following the dynamism of his
exaltation. Then one enters the world by admiring it. The world
is constituted by the totality of our admiration. And we are always coming upon the maxim of our admirative critique of poets:
admire first, then you will understand.

V

In the course of our previous works on the imagination of substances to which values have been given, we have very often encountered manifestations of the cosmic imagination, but we have
not always considered systematically enough the essential cosmicity which makes privileged images expand. In this chapter devoted to the cosmic imagination, we believe something would be
missing if we did not give some examples of this *image princeps*.
We shall take our examples from works which we have come to
know, alas! too late to support our theses on the imagination of
substance with them, but which encourage us to pursue our research on the phenomenology of the creative imagination. Isn't it
striking that, as soon as one dreams of images of high cosmicity

---

[38] Arthur Lundkvist, *Feu contre feu*, transcription from the Swedish by Jean-
Clarence Lambert, Paris, ed. Falaize, p. 43.

like images of fire, water, or the bird, he has evidence, by reading the poets, of an entirely new activity of the creative imagination?

Let us begin with a simple reverie before the fireplace. We are taking it from one of Henri Bosco's most profound books, *Malicroix*.

It is of course a question of the reverie of a solitary man, of a reverie free from the traditional image overload that one gets from a *family evening* around the hearth. Bosco's dreamer (*songeur*) is so phenomenologically solitary that psychoanalytical commentary would be *superficial*. Bosco's dreamer (*songeur*) is alone before the primordial fire.

The fire which burns in the hearth of *Malicroix* is a *fire of roots*. One does not dream in front of a fire of roots the same way he does in front of a fire of logs. The dreamer who puts a knotty root on the fire prepares for himself an accentuated reverie, a reverie with a double cosmicity, uniting the cosmicity of the root to the cosmicity of the fire. The images hold together: upon the strong coals of the hard wood *takes root* the short flame: "There climbed a living tongue which balanced in the black air like the very soul of fire. This creature lived at ground level on its old brick hearth. It lived there with patience; it had the tenacity of the little fires which last and slowly dig into the ash." [39] The ash seems to help them burn, these little fires which "dig into the ash," with rootlike slowness; the ash seems to be the humus which nourishes the stem of fire. [40]

"It was one of those fires," continues Henri Bosco, "of an ancient origin, which never ceased being nourished and whose life has persisted in the shelter of the ash upon the same hearth for innumerable years."

Yes, to what time, toward what memory are we carried by the dream (*songe*) before those fires which dig into the past as they "dig into the ash"? "These fires," says the poet, "have such a power

---

[39] Henri Bosco, *Malicroix*, Gallimard, p. 34.
[40] The roots burning in Malicroix's hearth are tamarisk roots. But it is only when the dreamer's well-being is accentuated that he will feel its "fragrant flame" (p. 37). In burning, the root will exhale the qualities of the flower. Thus, the union of the wood and the flame is consumed like a nuptial sacrifice. One dreams twice in front of a root fire.

over our memory that the immemorial lives dozing beyond the oldest memories awaken within us at their flame and reveal to us the furthest countries of our secret soul. Alone, on this side of the time which presides over our existence, they brighten days previous to our days and unknowable thoughts of which our thought is perhaps often only the shadow. In contemplating these fires associated with man by millenia of fire, one loses the feeling of the flight of things; time sinks into absence, and hours leave us with no jolt. What was, what is, what will be becomes by founding for itself the very presence of being; and nothing else in the enchanted soul distinguishes it from itself except perhaps the infinitely pure sensation of its existence. One affirms in no way that he is; but there still remains a faint gleam that he may be. Would I be? one murmurs to himself, and he no longer holds to the life of this world by anything but this hardly articulated doubt. The only human element that remains within us is warmth; for we no longer see the flame that communicates it. We are ourselves that familiar fire which has been burning at ground level since the dawn of the ages, but from which there always rises a living point above the hearth where the friendship of men keeps watch." [41]

We did not want to interrupt this great passage of gentle ontology, but it would be necessary to comment on it line by line to exhaust all its philosophical teachings. It sends us back to the *cogito* of the dreamer, of a dreamer who would be angry with himself for doubting his images in order to affirm his existence. The *cogito* of the dreamer in *Malicroix* opens to us the existence of an ante-existence. Time immemorial opens before us when we dream on the "childhood" of fire. All childhoods are the same: childhood of man, childhood of the world, childhood of fire are all lives which do not run along the thread of a history. The cosmos of the dreamer puts us in an immobile time; it helps us melt into the world. Warmth is within us, and we are in warmth, in a warmth equal to ourselves. Warmth (*chaleur*, f.) comes to bring the support of its feminine softness to the fire (*feu*, m.). Will a brutal metaphysics come to tell us that we are being thrown into the warmth, into the world of fire? Oppositional

---

[41] *Loc. cit.*, p. 35.

metaphysics can do nothing in the face of the evidence of reverie. In reading the passage by Bosco, the well-being of the world invades us from all directions. Everything melts together; everything is unified; well-being has the odor of tamarisk; the warmth is fragrant.

Starting from this repose in the well-being of an image, the writer makes us experience an expanding cosmos of repose. In another passage from *Malicroix*, Bosco writes: "Outside, the air reposed on the tips of trees and did not budge. Inside, the fire lived with prudence, in order to last till day. There escaped only the pure sentiment of being. Within me, no movement; my plans were at rest; my mental figures slumbered in the shadow." [42]

Out of time, out of space, before the fire, our being is no longer chained to a *being-there*, our I, to convince itself of its existence, of an existence which lasts, is no longer obliged to make strong affirmations, decisions which give us the future of energetic projects. Harmonious reverie has returned us to a harmonious existence. Ah! the gentle fluency of the reverie which helps us pour ourselves into the world, into the well-being of a world. Once more, reverie teaches us that the essence of being is well-being, a well-being rooted in the archaic being. Without *having been*, how can a philosopher be *sure of being?* The archaic being teaches me to be the same as myself. So constant, so prudent, so patient, the fire of *Malicroix* is a fire at peace with itself.

In front of this fire which teaches the dreamer the archaic and the intemporal, the soul is no longer stuck in a corner of the world. It is at the center of the world, at the center of its world. The simplest hearth encloses a universe. At least, that expanding movement is one of two metaphysical movements of reverie before fire. There is another which brings us back to ourselves. And thus it is that before the hearth, the dreamer is alternatively soul and body, body and soul. Sometimes the body takes up all the being. Bosco's dreamer knows those times of the dominating body: "Seated before the fire, I let myself go off into the contemplation of half burned logs, of flames and ashes until rather late. But nothing emerged from the hearth. The burning logs, flames

---

[42] Henri Bosco, *Malicroix*, p. 138.

and ashes obediently remained what they were and did not become (what they also are) mysterious marvels. Yet they pleased me, but more by their useful warmth than by their evocative force. I was not dreaming, I was getting warm. And getting warm is soft; it gives you a good notion of the body, the contact with yourself; and, if one imagines something, it is on the outside, the night, the cold, for one then curls up, snugly cared for, upon his own warmth." [43] The text is useful in its simplicity, for it teaches us to forget nothing. There are times when reverie digests reality, times when the dreamer incorporates his well-being, when he warms himself in depth. To be nice and warm is a way of dreaming for the body. And thus it is in reverie's two movements before the fire, the movement which makes us flow into a happy world and the movement which makes our body a sphere of well-being, Henri Bosco teaches us to warm ourselves body and soul. A philosopher who knew how to welcome the warmth of a fireplace that well would easily develop a metaphysics of adherence to the world which would be just the antithesis of the metaphysics which know the world by its oppositions. A fireplace dreamer can make no mistake: the world of warmth is the world of generalized softness. And for a word dreamer, warmth (*chaleur,* f.) is really, in all the depth of the term, fire in the feminine.

The *Malicroix* watch continues. Then comes the time when the fire dies down. There is no longer anything "but a fragment of warmth visible to the eye. No more steam, no crackling. The immobile glow took on a mineral aspect. . . . Was it living? But who was living, besides me and my solitary body?" By dying doesn't the fire erase our soul? We were living in such union with the soul of the glimmers of the hearth! Everything was glow within us and outside us. We were living from soft light, by soft light. The last glimmers of the fire have such tenderness! One believed himself to be two when he was alone. Half a world has been cut off from us.

What a lot of other pages would have to be meditated upon in order to understand that the fire *inhabits* the house. In the style of utility, one would say that the fire makes the house habitable.

---

[43] Henri Bosco, *Malicroix,* pp. 134–135.

This last expression belongs to the language of those who do not know the reveries of the verb "to inhabit." [44] The fire transmits its friendship in its entirety to the house and thus makes the House a Cosmos of warmth. Bosco knows that; he says as much: "The air dilated by warmth filled all the corners of the house, heavy upon the walls, the floor, the low ceiling, the heavy furniture. Life was circulating there, from the fire to the closed doors and from the doors to the fire, while tracing invisible circles of warmth which brushed my face. The odor of ashes and wood, led on by the movement of translation, made this life still more concrete. The least glimmers of flame trembled while feebly coloring the plaster partitions. A gentle humming, in which there was fused a thread of light steam, arose from the hearth at work. All these things formed a warm body whose penetrating softness invited one to repose and to friendship." [45]

Someone will object perhaps, in reading this passage, that the writer is no longer telling his reverie but describing his well-being in a closed room. But let us read better, let us read while dreaming, while remembering. The writer is speaking to us of ourselves, the dreamers, of ourselves, faithful to memory. The fire has kept us company too. We have known the friendship of fire. We communicate with the writer because we are comunicating with images preserved in the depths of ourselves. We return to dream in the rooms where we have known the friendship of fire. Henri Bosco reiterates for us all the duties implied by this friendship: "You must watch . . . and feed this simple fire with piety, with prudence. I have no other friend than he who warms the central stone of the house, the communicative stone whose warmth and light rise to my knees and to my eyes. There, the old pact of fire, the earth and the soul is sealed religiously between man and the refuge." [46]

All these reveries before the fire bear the great mark of simplicity. In order to live them in their simplicity, it is necessary to love repose. A great soul repose is the benefit of such reveries. There

---

[44] We have studied these reveries in our book, *The Poetics of Space,* (New York, 1964), Orion Press.
[45] Henri Bosco, *loc. cit.,* p. 165.
[46] Henri Bosco, *loc. cit.,* p. 220.

are, naturally, many other images to be put under the sign of fire. We hope to be able to take up all the images of fire in another work. In this book on reverie we only wish to show that in front of the fireplace, a dreamer experiences a reverie which *deepens*. Dreaming before the fire or before water, one knows a sort of stable reverie. Fire and water have a power of oneiric integration. Then the images have roots. In following them, we adhere to the world; we take root in the world.

By following a poet's reverie before still water, we are going to find new arguments for a metaphysics of the adherence to the world.

VI

Reveries before still water also bring us a great soul repose. More gently and, consequently, more surely than the reveries before too lively flames, these water reveries abandon the disordered fantasies of the imagination. They simplify the dreamer. With what facility these reveries become intemporal! How easily they link the spectacle with the memory! The spectacle or the memory? Is it really necessary *to see* tranquil water, to see it *right now*? For a word dreamer, the words "still water" (*eau dormante*) have a hypnotic softness. By dreaming a little, one comes to know that *all tranquility is still water*. There is still water at the bottom of all memory. And in the universe, still water is a mass of tranquility, a mass of immobility. In the still waters, the world rests. Before still water, the dreamer *adheres* to the repose of the world.

The lake and the pond are there. They are privileged with presence. Little by little, the dreamer is in this presence. In this presence, the dreamer's I knows opposition no longer. There is nothing more *against* him. The universe has lost all functions of *against*. The soul is at home everywhere in a universe which reposes on the pond. The still water integrates all things, the universe and its dreamer.

In this union, the soul meditates. It is near still water that the dreamer posits his *cogito* most naturally, a veritable *cogito* of the soul where the being of the depths is going to be assured. After a sort of forgetfulness of self which descends to the depths of being, without needing the gossip of doubt, the soul of the dreamer rises back to the surface to live its universe life. Where do those plants live which come to pose their broad leaves on the mirror of the waters? Where do those reveries come from, so fresh and so ancient? The mirror of the waters? It is the only mirror an interior life has. In tranquil water how close the surface and the depths are! Depth and surface are reconciled. The deeper the water, the clearer the mirror. Light emerges from the abysses. Depth and surface belong one to the other, and the reverie of still waters goes endlessly from one to the other. The dreamer dreams at his own depth.

Here again, Henri Bosco is going to help us give body to our dreams (*songes*). From the depths of "a lacustrian retreat," he writes: "Only there would I sometimes manage to climb back from the blackest of myself and forget myself. My interior vacuum would fill up. . . . The fluidity of my thought, in which I had until then vainly tried to find myself, appeared to me more natural and thus less bitter. I sometimes had the almost physical sensation of another underlying world whose substance, tepid and moving too, was flowering underneath the mournful expanse of my consciousness. And then, like the limpid water of the ponds, it shivered." [47] Thoughts passed over the mournful consciousness without being able to secure the being. Reverie fixes the being in communion with the being of deep water. The deep water contemplated in a reverie helps tell the deep soul of the dreamer. "Lost on the ponds," continues the writer, "I soon had the illusion of finding myself, no longer in a real world made up of silt, of birds, of plants and hardy shrubs, but in the very middle of a soul whose movements and times of calm became confused with my interior variations. And this soul resembled me. There, my mental life easily surpassed my thought. It was not an escape. . . . but an interior fusion." [48]

Ah! the word "fusion" is no doubt known to the philosophers. But the thing? How could we have the metaphysical experience of a "fusion" without the quality of an image? Fusion, total adherence to a substance of the world! Adherence of our whole being to some one of the many qualities of welcome in the world.

[47] Henri Bosco, *Hyacinthe*, Paris, Gallimard, p. 28.
[48] Henri Bosco, *Hyacinthe*, p. 29.

Bosco's dreamer has just told us how his dreamer's soul has melted into the soul of the deep water. . . . Bosco has really written a passage of universe psychology. If, following this model, a psychology of the universe could be developed in harmony with a psychology of reverie, how much better we would inhabit the world!

VII

The lake, the pond, the still water very naturally awaken our cosmic imagination through the beauty of a reflected world. When he is near such things, a dreamer receives a very simple lesson for imagining the world, for doubling the real world with an imagined world. The lake is a master at natural watercolors. The colors of the reflected world are tenderer, softer, more beautifully artificial than the heavily substantial colors. Already, those colors born by the reflections belong to an idealized universe. The reflections thus invite any dreamer of still water to idealization. The poet who goes to dream before water will not try to make it into an *imaginary painting*. He will always go a little beyond the real. Such is the phenomenological law of poetic reverie. Poetry continues the beauty of the world, aestheticizes the world. We are going to have new proofs of that by listening to the poets.

In the middle of one of his novels of extreme passion, D'Annunzio has situated a reverie before a limpid water where the soul comes to find its repose, repose in the dream of a love which could remain pure: "Between my soul and the landscape, there was a secret correspondence, a mysterious affinity. It seemed that the image of wood on the water of the ponds was really the dreamed image of the real scene. As in Shelley's poem, each pond seemed to be a narrow sky which had plunged into a subterranean world, a firmament of rose-colored light stretched out over the obscure earth, deeper than the deep night, purer than the day and where trees had developed in the same way as in the air above but with more perfect subtleties and tints than those which were waving in that place. And delicious views such as one never saw on the surface of our world were painted there by the love of the water for the beautiful forest; and, in all their depth, they were penetrated with an Elysian clarity, with an atmosphere without variations, with a sunset softer than ours." "From what distance of ages did that hour come to us!" [49]

The passage says everything: isn't it the water which *is dreaming* in this reverie? And in order to dream so faithfully, so tenderly in increasing the beauty of what is dreamed, isn't it necessary for the water of the pond to love "the beautiful forest?" Isn't this love shared? Doesn't the forest love the water which reflects its beauty? Isn't there a mutual adoration between the beauty of the sky and the beauty of the waters? [50] In its reflections, the world is twice beautiful.

From what distance of the ages comes that clarity of the Elysian souls? The poet would know if the new love which is inspiring him were not already on its way to following the fatality of loves devoted to voluptuousness. This hour is a memory of lost purity. For the water which "remembers" remembers those times. Whoever dreams before a limpid water dreams of the original purities. From the world to the dreamer, the water reverie experiences a communication of purity. How one would wish to begin his life all over, a life which would be the life or original dreams! Every reverie has a past, a distant past and, for certain souls, the water reverie is privileged with simplicity.

The redoubling of the sky in the mirror of the waters calls the reverie to a greater lesson. Isn't this sky enclosed in the water the image of a sky enclosed within our soul? This dream is excessive —but it has been dreamed; it was experienced by that great dreamer Jean-Paul Richter. Jean-Paul pushes the dialectic of the contemplated world and the world recreated by reverie to the absolute. Doesn't he wonder which is truer, the sky above our heads or the sky in the intimacy of a soul which is dreaming before a tranquil water? Jean-Paul does not hesitate in answering: "The interior sky restores and reflects the exterior sky which isn't really a sky." [51] The translator has weakened the text. It is neces-

---

[49] G. D'Annunzio, *L'enfant de volupté*, translated by Herrelle, p. 221.
[50] Sainte-Beuve himself—who rarely dreams—said in *Volupté:* "The firmament's moon admires in peace that of the waters."
[51] Jean-Paul Richter, *Le jubilé*, translated by Albert Béguin. (Paris, 1930), Stock, p. 176.

sary, writes Jean-Paul: *dass der innere Himmel den äusseren, der selten einer ist, erstatte, reflektiere, verbaue.*[52] For the dreamer in *Jubilee,* the constituting forces belong to the interior sky in the soul which dreams while looking at the world in the depths of the water. The word *verbaue* which has not been translated is the extreme word of *total* reversal. The world is not just reflected; it is not statically restored. It is the dreamer who expends his entire self in constituting the exterior sky. For a great dreamer, to see something in the water is to see it in his soul, and the exterior world is soon no more than what he has dreamed. This time, the real is no more than the reflection of the imagined.

It seems to us that a text this decisive by a dreamer as decided as Jean-Paul Richter opens the way to an ontology of the imagination. If we are sensitive to this ontology, an image given by a poet in passing encounters prolonged echoes within us. The image is new, always new, but the resonance is always the same. Thus, a simple image is a revealer of the World. Jean-Clarence Lambert writes: "The sun on the lake lingers like a peacock.[53] Such an image brings everything together. It is at the turning point where the world is alternatively spectacle or gaze. When the lake shivers, the sun gives it the sparkle of a thousand looks. The Lake is the Argus of its own Cosmos. All the beings of the World deserve words written with capital letters. The Lake makes the beautiful as the Peacock makes the wheel to display all the eyes of its plumage. Once more we have proof of the truth of our axiom of imagined cosmology: everything which sparkles sees. For a dreamer of the lake, water is the first look of the world. Yvan Goll writes in a poem entitled "Eye":

> I look at you looking at me: my eye
> Rises from I know not where
> To the surface of my face
> With the impertinent look of the lakes.[54]

52 *Der Jubelsenior, Ein Appendix* von Jean Paul, (Leipzig, 1797) J. G. Beigang, p. 364.
53 Jean-Clarence Lambert, *Dépaysage.* Paris, Falaize, p. 23.
54 Yvan Goll, *Les cercles magiques.* Paris, Falaize, p. 41.

The psychology of the imagination of reflections before a limpid water is so varied that it would be necessary to write a whole book to distinguish all its elements. Let us give a single example where the dreamer gives himself over to an imagination which is joking. We shall take this reverie which is having fun from Cyrano de Bergerac. A nightingale sees its image on the mirror of the waters: "The nightingale who, from high on a branch, looks at himself in there (the waters) and believes he has fallen into the river. . . . He warbles, he explodes, he bawls, and that other nightingale, without breaking the silence, apparently bawls like him and deceives the heart with so much charm that one imagines he is bawling only to make himself heard by our eyes." [55] Pushing his game further, Cyrano writes: "The pike who is looking for him, touches him and can not feel him, runs after him and is astonished to have pierced him through so many times. . . . It is a visible nothing, a night that the night makes die."

A physicist will have a fine time trying to denounce the illusion of the pike, who, like a dream (*songe*) philosopher, believes he can nourish himself with "virtual" images. But when a poet begins to tell all his fantasies, it is not for the physicist to stop him.

VIII

In order to give a concrete example of a universe psychology, we are going to follow an account where the décor of a mountain lake in some way creates its character, where the strong, deep water, provoked by swimming, transforms a human being into a water being—transforms a woman into Mélusine. Our commentary will center on Jacques Audiberti's great book, *Carnage*.

Audiberti only occasionally gives reflection images. His reverie is attracted by water as if his imagination had the powers of hydromancy, the attractions of hydrophilia. The dreamer dreams of living in the thickness of the water. He will live from tactile *images*. The imagination will no longer give us only a beyond of contemplated images, but a beyond of the muscular joys, a beyond of the forces of swimming. In reading the pages Jacques Audiberti wrote in a chapter bearing the title "The Lake," [56] one

---

[55] Quoted by Adrien de Meeüs, *Le romantisme.* (Paris, 1948), Fayard, p. 45.
[56] Jacques Audiberti, *Carnage.* (Paris, 1942), Gallimard, p. 36. Cf. pp. 49–50.

could at first believe that they express positive experiences, but each sensation noted is increased in an image. We are entering into the region of a poetics of the perceptible. And if there is experience, it is of a veritable imagination experience that one must speak. Naked reality would mute this experience of the poetics of the perceptible. From then on, such prowesses in the life of water must not be read by referring them to our experiences, to our memories; they must be read *imaginatively,* by participating in the poetics of the perceptible, in the poetics of tactility, the poetics of muscular tonality. We shall note in passing those psychological ornaments which give an aesthetic life to simple perceptions. First let us introduce the heroine of the world of the waters.

Audiberti dreams directly of the forces of nature. He does not need legends and tales to create a Mélusine. As long as she is living on land, his Mélusine is a village girl. She speaks, she lives as the villagers do. But the lake makes her *alone* and from the time she is alone near the lake, the lake becomes a universe. The village girl enters the green water, a morally green water, sister of the intimate substance of a Mélusine. And now she is diving: foam emerges from a whirlpool whitening the intimacy of the liquid world with a thousand hawthorn flowers. The swimmer is now beneath the waves: "Henceforth, nothing existed other than an ecstasy of rustling (*rumeur*) bluer than anything in the world. . . ." [57]

"An ecstasy of rustling bluer than anything in the world." To what perceptible register does this image belong? Let the psychologist decide; but the word dreamer is delighted, for the reverie of the waters here is a spoken reverie. Here, the poetics of the word is the dominant poetics. It is necessary to repeat and repeat again in order to hear all that the poet is saying. For the ear which wants to hear the voice of the waves, what a seashell is the word "*rumeur.*"

The writer continues: " . . . (the swimming girl) moved through the interior of the liquid azurage. . . . Tied to the blue water which surrounds her, fills her, and dissolves her, she re-

---

[57] Jacques Audiberti, *Carnage*, p. 49.

corded the claps of black thunder which the infused day designs beneath the waves." In the bosom of the waters there is born another sun; light has eddies; it propagates dizzinesses. Whoever sees beneath the water must often shield his retina. With each stroke, the world of the waters changes its violence. The ardent Mélusine, says Jacques Audiberti, "wound to her body those rosaries of a furious universe where there is expressed the breathing of invisible horses who are sheltered by the marvel." For the poet—it is his function—must give us worlds of marvel, those worlds which are born from an exalted cosmic image. And this time thanks to exaltation, the cosmic image is not purely and simply drawn from the world; it surpasses the world in some way beyond all that is perceived. Audiberti writes of his swimmer: "Into the sparkling night of the waters, lacustrian night, favorable night, she reentered, traveled, meditated, *far beyond the powers of swimming.*" [58]

But universes so new, so strongly imagined cannot help but work on the being which is imagining them in its substratum. If we follow the images of the poet in all sincerity, it seems to us that the imagination destroys a being of the earth within us. We are tempted to let a being of water be born in us. The poet has invented a being; so it is possible to invent beings. For each invented world, the poet causes an inventing subject to be born. He delegates his power to invent to the being he invents. We enter the realm of the *cosmicizing I*. Thanks to the poet, we relive the dynamism of an origin within us and outside us. A phenomenon of being with a basis in reverie arises beneath our eyes and fills that reader with light who accepts the impulsions of the poet's image. Audiberti's Mélusine experiences a change of being; she destroys a human nature in order to receive a cosmic nature. "She ceases to be, in order to be much more . . . reconciled to the glory of abolishing herself without, however, dying." [59] Melting into the basic element is a necessary human suicide for whoever wants to experience an emergence into a new cosmos. Forgetting the earth and disavowing our earthly being is a double necessity for whoever loves water with a cosmic love. Then, there is nothing before

---

[58] *Loc. cit.* p. 56. Our italics.
[59] Jacques Audiberti, *Carnage*, p. 60.

water. Above water, there is nothing. Water is the whole world. What a drama of ontologies the poet calls us to live! What a new life it is when events are called into being by images! In coming to the lake, Mélusine "broke with each and every form of social destiny. She filled the cup of nothingness with nature. In suicide, she became immense. But when, bathed to the bottom of her heart, she came back to the world and its drying out, she almost felt that she was the water of the lake. The water of the lake arises. It walks." [60] Coming back onto land, walking on the ground, Mélusine kept the energy of swimming. In her, water is a being of energy. In Audiberti's water heroine, one can say, using a line by Tristan Tzara, that "soft water and muscled water" met.[61]

That water which "arises," that upright water, that standing water, what a new being!

There, we are touching squarely on one extremity of reverie. Since the poet dares to write this extreme reverie, the reader must dare to read it to the point of a kind of beyond of reader's reveries, without reticence, without reduction, without worry about "objectivity," even adding, if it is possible, his own fantasy to the fantasy of the writer. Reading always at the summit of the images, stretched toward the desire to surpass the summits, will give the reader well-defined exercises in phenomenology. The reader will know imagination in its essence since he will be living it in its excess, in the absolute of an incredible image, the sign of an extraordinary being.

In habitual reveries on water, in the classical psychology of water, nymphs were not, everything considered, extraordinary beings. One could imagine them as beings of the mist, as water spirits (eaux "follettes"), flexible sisters of the fires which run across the surface of the pond. The nymphs only realize a subaltern human promotion. They remained beings of gentleness, of softness, of whiteness. Mélusine contradicts facile substance. She is a water who wishes verticality, a hard and vigorous water. She belongs more to a poetics of the reverie of forces than to a poetics of the

60 Jacques Audiberti, loc. cit., p. 50.
61 Tristan Tzara, Parler seul, ed. Caractères, p. 40.

reverie of substance. We are going to have evidence of that by reading further in that great book, *Carnage*.

IX

In an imagined, imaginary cosmic life, the different worlds often touch each other and complement each other. The reverie of one calls up the reverie of the other. In a previous work,[62] we assembled numerous documents which prove the oneiric continuity which unites dreams of swimming with dreams of flight. Already, by the pure mirror of the lake, the sky becomes an aerial water. The sky is then, for the water, the call to a communion in the verticality of being. The water which reflects the sky is a depth of the sky. This double space mobilizes all the values of cosmic reverie. As soon as a being who dreams without limit, a dreamer open to all dreams (*songes*) lives intensely in one of the two spaces, he also wants to live in the other. Through his dreams (*songes*) of swimming, Audiberti has succeeded in creating a water so dynamic, a water so well "muscled" that the Mélusine of the waters dreams of forces which, in a dive to the bottom of the sky, would give her the being of a Mélusine of the air. She wants to fly. She dreams of beings which fly. How often, at the edge of the lake, Mélusine has contemplated the hawk tracing circles around the zenith! Aren't the rounds in the sky the images of rounds which run along the surface of the sensitive river at the least breeze? The world is one.

The reveries unite, fuse together. The winged being which turns in the sky and the waters which are going on their whirls[63] make an alliance. But it is the hawk that turns the best. What do the hawks dream about, sleeping up there as they turn? Aren't they, they too, like the philosopher's Moon, carried away by a whirlpool. Yes, what do philosophers dream about when the water images *immediately* become thoughts of the sky? And the dreamer endlessly follows the astronomic voyage of the hawk. What glory, what prestige of flight is that circle so well traced

---

62 Cf. *L'air et les songes*, Corti, Chap. I.
63 "Whirls" translates *tourbillons* which can mean either "whirlpool" or "whirlwind" (Translator's note).

around the zenith! Swimming knew only the straight line. It is necessary to fly like the hawk in order to understand concretely the geometry of the cosmos.

But let us be less of a philosopher and take up our apprenticeship in the psychological art of dynamogeny again by following the lessons of the poet's reverie.

Thus, Mélusine dreams twice, always twice—in the azure of the sky and in the somber blue of the lake. Then Audiberti writes great pages of dynamized psychology on the attempted flight, on the realized flight, on the failed flight. First, there are the convictions acquired in the dreams of the night, oneiric convictions which find themselves prepared or confirmed by the reverie of alleviation which does not leave Mélusine's mind during the day: "Sometimes, with her eyes closed, lying in the grass or on her bed, she would attempt to escape from weights. One emerges from his body to the light pilgrimage by what is indomitable in him. One situates himself, with force, in the air above his remains—and, yet, these remains, your flesh, you are carrying it away with you, but deboned, depoisoned. One night she even thought she was succeeding. She felt herself being born toward the ceiling. She was not touching anymore either with her back or her feet or her stomach. She was rising gently. . . . Was she dreaming? Was she not dreaming? Yet she grasped the beam with her left hand. Before coming back down, she could tear away three slivers of light wood, certain evidence. And then she fell back—fell back!—into sleep. On waking, the three slivers of wood had disappeared." [64]

Here, the imagining writer is a precise psychologist. He knows that, in the dream of flight, the dreamer is filled with objective proofs. The dreamer tears a splinter of wood from the ceiling, he picks a leaf from the top of the tree, he takes an egg from the nest of the crow. To these precise facts are united well-connected reasonings, well-chosen arguments to be given to those who do not know how to fly. On waking, alas, the proofs are no longer in his hands; the good reasons are no longer in his mind.

But the benefit of the nocturnal dream of lightness remains. Reverie takes up the germ of aerial being formed in the night.

---

[64] Jacques Audiberti, *loc. cit.*, pp. 56–57.

Reverie nourishes it, no longer with proofs, no longer with experiences, but with images. Here, once more, the images can do anything. When a happy impression of lightening comes into the soul, it also comes to the body and, for an instant, life has a destiny of images.

To feel oneself light is so concrete a sensation!—so useful, so precious, so humanizing! Why don't the psychologists worry about setting up a pedagogy of this lightness of being for us? So it becomes the poet's duty to teach us to incorporate the impressions of lightness into our lives, to give body to impressions too often neglected. For that, too, let us follow Audiberti.

As soon as Mélusine, with a light step, has climbed the gentle slope of the hill, she flies: "Intoxicated with so many skies eaten like seeds, seeds of the azure elixir which makes one fly, she walks, she is still walking, but already she is sprouting wings, black wings of night, cut out by the spiny ridge of the mountains. No! the mountains themselves are part of the substance of these wings, the mountains with their mountain pastures, their little houses, their spruce trees. . . . She permits these wings to live, to beat. They are going to beat. They do beat. She walks, she is flying. She stops walking. She flies. She is everywhere that which flies. . . ." [65]

One must read these pages in a great tension of reading, believing what he reads. The writer wants to convince the reader of the reality of the cosmic forces in action in the images of flight. He has a faith which, still greater than that which moves mountains, makes them fly. Aren't the summits wings? In his call to a sympathy of the imagination, the writer harries the reader, he dogs him. It seems to me that I hear the poet saying: "Won't you ever fly away, reader! Are you going to stay there seated, inert, while a whole universe is stretched toward the destiny of flying?"

Ah! books too have their own reveries. Each of them has a tonality of reverie, for each reverie has a particular tonality. If one is too often unaware of the individuality of a reverie, it is because he has decided to hold reverie to be a confused psychic state. But books which dream correct this error. Then the books are our real masters in dreaming. Without a total sympathy with

---

[65] Jacques Audiberti, *loc. cit.*, p. 63.

reading, why read? But when one really enters the book's reverie, how can he stop reading?

Then as one pursues his reading of Audiberti's book, his eyes open: he sees flight conquer the world. The world must fly. There are so many beings which live by flying that flight is surely the next destiny of the sublimated world: " . . . so many birds, the little ones and the fat, and the brushing dragonfly and the mica-winged *semblide,* "half as long as his female. Yes, the universe is a lake. Trampling along the floor of this lake with her knees a little low, as she is doing now, she feels shame." [67] Then, ceaselessly, it is necessary to begin again the whole process which will bear the dreaming girl into the azure of the sky. A being who can fly must not remain on the ground: "It is necessary that, once and for all, she fly away. She must melt and swim and cut through the air. Fly, girl of nothing, lonely soul, obscure candle . . . Fly! . . . She flies. . . . Substances alter. A gust as heavy as waves supports her. She reaches bird power. She dominates." [68]

But in the extreme success comes the collapse. The reverie comes to earth. An immense regret "trembles in the bells of defeat" which sound the swoon of a being falling back from such a dream into reality. "Won't she ever fly? From the essence of air to the essence of water is the distance that great?" Is it possible that so great, so strong, so stirring a reverie can be contradicted by reality? It fused so well to life, to our life! It so surely gave life to a flight of life! It had given so much being to our imagining being! For us, it had been an opening onto a world so new, so far above the world worn by daily life!

Ah! at least, however weak our imaginary wings may be, the reverie of flight opens a world to us; it is opening onto the world, a great opening, a wide opening. The sky is the window of the world. The poet teaches us how to hold it wide open.

In spite of the numerous long excerpts we have taken from Jacques Audiberti's book, we have not been able to follow the reverie of the air in all its stirrings and in all its resumptions; we

---

[66] What a lot of other birds there are which make crystal and all the other minerals of the earth fly to the sky!

[67] *Loc. cit.,* p. 63.

[68] *Loc. cit.,* p. 64.

have not been able to tell all the peripeteiae of a dialectic which goes from the liquid universe to the aerial universe. In breaking up our quotations we have broken with the enthusiasm of the text with the poetic enthusiasm of images which, in spite of their riches and their fantasy, conquer *a unity of reverie.* Yet we would wish to have convinced our reader of the increase of psychic power which the poet's art brings to the simple account of the events of a dream. A poetic unity comes to graft itself onto the unity of reverie.

If a Poetics of Reverie could be constructed, it would uncover examination procedures which would allow us to study the activity of the imagination systematically. From the example which we have just set forth, one would thus draw a series of questions to ask in order to determine the possibilities of adherence to the poetry of images. Poetic values make the reverie psychically beneficial. Through poetry, reverie becomes positive, becomes an activity which ought to interest the psychologist.

Without following the poet into his deliberately *poetic* reverie, how will one make up a psychology of the imagination? Will he take documents from those who do not imagine, who forbid themselves to imagine, who "reduce" the abundant images to a stable idea, from those—more subtle negators of the imagination —who "interpret" images, ruining all possibility of an ontology of images and a phenomenology of the imagination at the same time?

What would the great dreams of the night be if they were not supported, nourished, poetized by the beautiful reveries of happy days? How would a dreamer of flight recognize his nocturnal experience in the passage which Bergson devotes to it.[69] Bergson, in explaining this dream, like several others, by psycho-physiological causes, does not appear to envisage the proper action of the imagination. For him, the imagination is not an autonomous psychological reality. Here then are the physical conditions which, according to him, cause the dream of flight. From your oneiric flight "if you awaken abruptly, here, I believe, is what you will find. You were feeling that your feet had lost their point of contact

[69] Henri Bergson, *L'énergie spirituelle*, Alcan, p. 90.

since, in fact, you were stretched out. On the other hand, believing that you were not sleeping, you had no knowledge of being in bed. So you said to yourself that you were no longer touching the ground, even though you were standing. It is this conviction which your dream developed. Notice, in the cases when you felt yourself flying, that you believe your body to be on its side, turned to the right or the left, while raising it with a sharp movement of your arm which would be like the beat of a wing. Now, this side is precisely the one on which you are lying. If you wake up you will find that the sensation of an effort to fly is identical with the sensation of the pressure of your arm and your body against the bed. The latter sensation, detached from its cause, was no longer anything more than a vague feeling of fatigue, attributable to an effort. Attached back then to the conviction that your body had left the ground, it is determined to be the precise feeling of an effort to fly."

Many points in this corporal "description" could give rise to controversy. Often the dream of flight is a dream without wings. The little wings at Mercury's heels are sufficient to provide the propulsion. It is very difficult to attach the delights of nocturnal flight back to the fatigue of an arm stuck in the bedding. But our major criticism is not addressed to these badly reported corporal facts. What is lacking in Bergson's explanation are the virtues of the living image, life in total imagination. In this domain, poets know more than philosophers.

X

By following, in the last paragraphs of this chapter, various reveries of escape which start from privileged images of fire, water, air, winds and flight, we have taken advantage of images which dilate by themselves, propagate themselves to the point of becoming images of the World. One could ask us to study images which are under the sign of the fourth element, the terrestrial element, in the same spirit. But, by making such a study, we would be abandoning the perspectives of the present work. We would no longer be dealing with reveries of the tranquility of being, with reveries of our idleness. In order to do research on what one can call the psychology of substances, it is necessary to think, to will.

We have often encountered reveries which think in the studies we have undertaken in order to "understand" alchemy. Then we were trying our hand at a mixed comprehension, at a comprehension which would welcome images and ideas, contemplations and experiences at the same time. But this mixed comprehension is impure and whoever wants to follow the extraordinary development of scientific thought must break definitively with the bonds of the image and the concept. We have made numerous efforts in our philosophical teaching to put this decision into practice. Among others we have written a book subtitled *Contribution to a Psychoanalysis of Objective Knowledge.* And more particularly, on the problem of the evolution of knowledge touching on matter, we have tried to show in our book, *Rational Materialism,* how the alchemy of the four elements in no way prepared the way for the knowledge of modern science.[70]

Thus, from all this past of culture, it remains true for us that the images of substances are touched by a polemic between imagination and thought. We were not supposed to think then of taking up its examination again in a book devoted to simple reverie.

Of course, reveries before the substances of the earth also have their relaxation. The dough which one kneads puts a gentle reverie into his fingers. Those reveries have held our attention long enough in the books we have written on the substances of the earth so that we shall not undertake an examination of them again in this work.

Beside those reveries which think, beside those reveries which offer themselves as thoughts, there are also reveries which wish; and I might add that they are very comforting reveries, very comforting because they prepare a wish. We have gathered together many types of them in the book we entitled precisely *The Earth and the Reveries of the Will.* Such reveries of the will prepare and support the energy for work. In studying poetics, one would encounter workers' songs. These reveries magnify the trade. They

[70] Cf. 1. *La formation de l'esprit scientifique. Contribution à une psychanalyse de la connaissance objective.* Vrin; 2. *Le matérialisme rationnel,* P. U. F.

put the trade in the Universe. The pages we have devoted to the reveries of the forge were trying to prove the cosmic destiny of the great trades.

But the outlines we were able to make in our book *The Earth and the Reveries of the Will* should be expanded. Above all, they should be taken up again in order to put all the trades in the movement of the life of our time. What a book then would have to be written to put the reveries of the will on a level with today's trades! One could no longer be satisfied with poor manual pedagogies where one marvels at seeing a child take interest in work-toys. Man has just entered a new maturity. So the imagination must serve the will, awaken the will to entirely new perspectives. And thus it is that a reverie dreamer cannot be satisfied with customary reveries. What joy one would have if he could detach himself from a book which is ending to take up another! But in such a desire the genders must not be confused. Reveries of the will must not come to brutalize, masculinize the reveries of leisure.

And since, when one ends a book, it is accepted practice to refer back to the hopes he cherished as he was beginning it, I see clearly that I have maintained all my reveries in the facilities of the *anima*. Since it was written in *anima*, we would wish that this simple book be read in *anima*. But just the same, so that it may not be said that the *anima* is the being of our whole life, we would still want to write another book which, this time, would be the work of an *animus*.